GAMEBOOK

(how not to change or improve yourself at all)

By Toe

Foreword by Trevor Sabourin, M.D.

Foreword

It's winter of 2015. I'm a medical student starting the first day of my month-long rotation in palliative care (a rotation that I specifically chose to experience).

What is palliative care? Most people in medicine would say it's the field of medicine that cares for those who are dying. People in palliative care would say they care for those who are *imminently* dying. When surrounded by all that death, one remembers: We are all dying.

I chose this elective because I thought a doctor should be an expert in all aspects of health (death included), and up until that point, I had only seen dead bodies in the anatomy lab. I had never even seen anyone pronounced dead. How is a doctor supposed to do that anyways? Someone who watches *Grey's Anatomy* (2005) probably knew more than I did about dying. Even medicine hides their death and dying, sweeping it under the metaphorical rug. Fortunately, I knew where "under the rug" was, and the undertakers agreed to teach me the ropes.

It's the first day. I'm a whirlwind of excitement and nerves (not uncommon for a medical student starting a new rotation). Today I will be in the trenches giving direct care to patients in a field of medicine that I know absolutely nothing about. Trial by fire. My fate for the next month rides on the guidance of the "death doctors" on the floor. Fortunately, they seem nice. In fact, everyone seems exceptionally nice. All that dying hasn't dampened their spirits. This is a little unexpected for me, as deaths on the other medical floors (not that I was involved in any of them) often got the staff down in the dumps for weeks.

The two doctors on that day divvy up some patients for me. Given that I'm a lowly "med 3," I'm assigned three patients. Great. OK. Let's read their charts and get up to date. The butterflies in my stomach are turning, and reading their charts just makes it worse. Each one is worse than the last. Riddled with cancer. Bed bound. Pain that worsens every day. Gasping for air. Oh and look… The last one's cancer weakened his spine so badly that he broke his neck by simply turning his head last week, and is now a quadrapalegic. What a sad lot they must be. How can I possibly help them?

I know! I have all the tools of modern medicine at my disposal, and no one cares what goes on in palliative care anyways. I'll offer to pump them full of drugs and send them off in an anesthetic coma. Numbness is the gift I can give them. With a plan in hand, I summon the courage to provide whatever care is possible. I commit and visit the worst of the worst, ready to present my offer.

What transpired over the next week changed my life forever. My three patients, physically best described as meat carcases, were obviously the most alive people I have ever seen. I was never able to offer them numbness; they were too busy trying to teach me how to feel. Each, in their own way, spent hours describing magic everywhere that I couldn't see. It was clear that their perspective shifts were a direct result of dying, but they assured me that it didn't have to be. Dying was literally the time of their lives and they wanted to share it with the living.

I spent as much time as possible with my patients, who were always greedy to share their insights. Some medicine did get done, but I frankly don't remember any of it. At their ends, the patients requested I be involved in each of their last conversations (one of whom, having no family of his own, simply asked for me). The families—often very uncomfortable with the whole dying thing—loved having the experts around, and were just as greedy to have me there as I was to be included. It seemed like all parties involved were trying to get something out of the experience.

When my patients passed, I pronounced each of them dead. I didn't study how one is *supposed* to do it. I simply laid my hands on the body of my friend and waited. It was obvious. It was sad. It was beautiful. Thank you.

My patients never met each other. They were not aware of the nearly identical nature of their individual discoveries, nor were they the only ones telling me similar stories during my time spent under the rug. Although I didn't get it at the time, I knew something was afoot. How were they all arriving at this same conclusion, and more importantly, what was it? They were clearly trying to tell me something, and felt it was important enough to spend their dying breaths on it. With my friends now gone and their words left echoing in my mind, I started down the path they pointed me toward.

Years later, a lone pilgrim pops out of the jungle for the second time, and is experiencing a particularly lucid period. The doctor tells his younger brother, as best he can, about what he has seen. His brother, the wordsmith of the family, doesn't quite get it, but knows there must be a reason to want to share whatever it is with such enthusiasm. The pointed out path now calls him too, and he decides to play along and dip his toe into the unknown.

Table of Nonsense

Introduction..9
Game A
    What is Game A?..13
    A1. I'm not good enough and I must improve.................17
    A2. White must win over black...............................21
    A3. This isn't a game...27
    A4. Lost in the sauce...33
    A5. The habit (I can do things)..............................41
    A6. The blue pill...45
    Game A summary..53
Game B
    What is Game B?..55
    B1. Full expression..59
    B2. Yin yang..65
    B3. What a ride/show..73
    B4. Smelling the roses...81
    B5. The weather...89
    B6. The red pill..95
    Game B summary...105
The Jungle
    What is the Jungle?...107
    J1. Fake Game B..111
    J2. House of cards..119
    J3. Running out of road.......................................127
    J4. Grasping at smoke..133
    J5. But how? (still the habit)................................139
    J6. The tough pill to swallow...............................147
    The Jungle summary...151
    J7. The way out...155
The Thing...159
Game C..163
Conclusion..167
Glossary..175
Media...177

Introduction

I have nothing to teach you. Take me at face value. More importantly, this book is most effective when enjoyed with a beverage of your choice. I recommend taking a break and preparing one now. If you have a nice drink prepared, treat yourself to a sip. If you aren't able to prepare one at the moment, then stop and reflect on my annoying instructions. If you ignored my annoying instructions, then I see you brought your A game... You win this round.

It's winter of 2019. I'm explaining to my brother that I'm sure I've seen what he's been trying to show me. I've got it all figured out. Life is just a big game, and the point of it all is to play it as playfully as possible. I recite an elaborate metaphor about parachutes that I've constructed to prove my understanding of enlightenment. He smiles and acknowledges my insight, then tries to take me one level deeper. He asks if I can see how if I had an infinite number of skydive jumps called "life," then I would want to experience crippling mental illness. The question confuses me into a tailspin. Wanting mental illness? Huh?? I thought it was all about playfulness, and who said anything about multiple jumps? Back to the drawing board I went, and the results of that process are laid out in the pages ahead. Did I manage to figure it all out? Can it be figured out with any degree of certainty? Are you capable of figuring out what I'm rambling about? I'll let you be the judge. Good luck.

What is it you're wishing to get out of this book? Perhaps you're like Neo in *The Matrix* (1999), and feel like something isn't quite right with the game you're playing. If you're searching for answers in the code of this game, I might be able to spell it out for you. I've tried to simplify my explanations of what I consider to be the game that most of us play, and want to stress that there are alternative games available to you.

You may find some of the concepts and non-concepts explored in this book challenging, but it would be a lot less fun if they weren't. Some of these ideas are fun to chew on, while others are less fun when they're chewing on you. I struggled with some episodes of anxiety while writing some of the more mind-bending sections. If you ever find yourself feeling unpleasantly ungrounded, then take a deep breath and take a break. Think of it like a passing storm.

Putting up with my nonsense can be challenging (just ask my friends). If you find something repetitive, it's because I feel it's worth repeating. If you find a contradiction, it's because I don't know what I'm talking about. If you find I'm being overly evasive and metaphorical, it's because I saw a Zen master do it one time and thought it was cool. We're well into the introduction, and I haven't really introduced what this book is about yet.

I'm not here to pave the roads and paint lines on them for you. I'm here to drop a few signposts in the jungle and point out some shortcuts I found in there. I'm reluctant to call what I have to offer "guidance," since I can't walk your path. I don't know where my next steps will be, so don't ask me to point out yours. I can't show you the things I want you to see, but I may be able to engage your curiosity enough for you to discover them on your own.

Some of those whom I've walked with and pointed in general directions have returned months—even years—later with incredible insights to share (some of which are in this book). I would not be writing this god-forsaken paperweight if I didn't have faith in the value of this process. I'm a massive hypocrite for writing it at all, but here we are.

Maybe we can walk together for a while and see how things play out. Maybe I'll be sharing some of your profound "parachute" insights in my next book (I'm not writing another book). Maybe you can take some of these ideas and improve them, or use them to improve yourself. Maybe not.

Game A

The way things are

The way things *could* be

Illustration by PlagueWerewolf (DeviantArt)

What is Game A?

Game A is a progress-driven worldview so pervasive that its players see it as the only game in town.

I've listed below what I feel are the six pillars of Game A, which will be explored in this section. The first three are the most overt and recognizable aspects of this game, while the others are more subtle and tend to operate in the background. Most of the concepts ahead should sound pretty familiar, but you may find it eye opening to see them defined and put under a microscope.

Game A pillars:

1. I'm not good enough and I must improve
2. White must win over black
3. This isn't a game
4. Lost in the sauce
5. The habit (I can do things)
6. The blue pill

Game A language tends to be action-oriented. Messaging is often punctuated by a call to action ('work, sweat, achieve,' 'rise and grind,' 'just do it,' etc.). I often walk by a gym where loud pop music is played and an instructor yells at students:

- "Dig deep!"
- "Work hard!"
- "Push through!"
- "You can do it!"

I'm always struck by how this language differs from what I hear at a yoga class:

- "You can play around with this variation."
- "Don't worry about what the posture looks like."
- "Honor any movement that you're craving."
- "Come out of it if it doesn't feel right."

This gym class no doubt ends with the teacher congratulating the students for "doing a great job," while my yoga class ends with "namaste," commonly translated as "the light in me honors the light in you." While both are different spins on "I see you," namaste implies no chore or job done. Perhaps this is why yoga is "practiced," and not completed like a task. Why do we go to the gym? To *work* out.

This prioritizing of action results in the worship of idols who have accomplished difficult feats or help others do great things.

Game A gods:

- Batman
- Elon Musk
- Jeff Bezos
- Bill Gates
- Steve Jobs
- Dwayne Johnson
- Tiger Woods
- Serena Williams
- David Goggins
- Joe Rogan
- Kim Kardashian
- Oprah Winfrey
- Tony Robbins
- Gary Vaynerchuk
- Jordan Peterson
- Mahatma Gandhi
- Mother Teresa
- Olympians
- Doctors
- Lawyers
- Scientists
- Celebrities

You may think this is totally obvious and wonder who we might idolize instead of these great doers. Notice how when you introduce yourself at a party, one of the first questions that comes up is "what do you do?" Our sense of self worth is strongly tied to our performance; we are what we do. We place the "successful" and the "winners" on a pedestal, and look down upon the "failures" and the "losers."

This game is usually learned at such an early age that it's difficult for adults to remember what came before it. Those who spend the vast majority of their lives playing it tend to grow extremely invested in it and attached to it. It becomes such an old habit that it usually takes a major life event to break it, such as a mid-life crisis, a spiritual awakening, or a terminal illness diagnosis. Such events share a common feature: Loss of control. Not being able to do anything is extremely frustrating for the doing-oriented mind, which even frames "surrendering" as another action for us to add to our to-do lists.

On top of all that action, Game A language tends to feature a heavy focus on change, progress, and improvement. Someone playing this game might feel like they're never getting enough juice for the squeeze they're putting in. Since they're always chasing more juice, messaging like "new and improved," "leveling up," or "optimize your life" resonates with them. Even if things are going great for them, things could always be *better*.

A1. I'm not good enough and I must improve

There's always stuff to work on. You're never there.

— Tiger Woods

The belief that "I'm not good enough and I must improve" is the most recognizable facet of Game A. This game is so incredibly pervasive that it appears to be the driving force behind nearly everything we say, think, and do. Think I'm exaggerating? Consider why you might want a better job, better appearance, better relationships, or better health. The desire to improve ourselves, others, or society is the foundation of Game A and its guiding North Star. Is there a desire to improve behind wanting to eat a cookie? Probably not. However, you might feel guilty for treating yourself to it, out of a desire to improve your health. You might have to look for it, but this drive is almost always fueling our behavior or beliefs in some form. It's sort of like clouds on an overcast day, in that it's ubiquitous to the point of near-invisibility.

When I shine a spotlight on this improvement instinct, people are usually able to see it driving various aspects of their life. However, most people have been playing this game so hard and for so long that they're convinced it's the only game in town. They equate it with life itself, and don't have the slightest clue how to stop playing it (in the same way they wouldn't know how to survive without eating or breathing). They can't imagine what the alternative would look like, or why you would want to pursue anything else. This game is so widely taught and played that it could be seen as the human condition itself. I believe it's the zeitgeist of our age (and has been for centuries, if not millennia). Cats stalk their prey, the sun sets in the west, and people play the improvement game. It's just what we do.

If you still think my claim is overly bold, I again invite you to look for signs of this game in yourself and your peers. Why do we make new laws? Why do we send our kids to school? Why do we celebrate our achievements? Why are you reading this book? Even if you are reading this book purely because you enjoy it, or put the book down and go to a party for the fun of it, consider whether you're pursuing these leisure activities out of a sense of what your "best self" should be doing. I can't count the number of times my mother has stressed that I *must* "get ahead." She is totally sincere in this belief that "getting ahead" is of critical importance, and is genuinely trying to help with that advice. When I ask *why* I must get ahead, she has no answer. Moms are always right though, so maybe I shouldn't question her.

I tend to question any advice that I should live another way than I already am. For example, telling someone that they are overweight or underweight is telling them they're supposed to be something other than what they are. Then we're surprised when people dislike their bodies. We'd likely never look at a cloud and think that it's misshapen, yet we look in the mirror every day and think that our bodies are misshapen. It saddens me to think how many people must genuinely believe that they're broken and need to be fixed. So many of us wish to belong to some sort of cool kid club of impressively improved people, but our wish to belong is a bold claim that we don't already. If the clouds are all perfectly shaped and placed, then why can't we be? Who knows… Maybe the clouds are up there judging each other and trying to "get in shape" because they've "let themselves go."

Story Time: The Personal Trainer

Anne is looking to shed some winter weight and get her beach body ready for summer. She hasn't had much luck with diets and gym memberships, but she hears whispers about an amazing personal trainer who makes house calls. This trainer, Marie, is expensive, but has a reputation for getting results and can accommodate Anne's irregular schedule.

Anne anxiously books her first session with Marie for the following week, but upon arriving home from work that evening, she finds Marie there waiting for her, and she clearly means business. Without bothering to exchange pleasantries, Marie launches Anne into a grueling workout, knowing exactly which muscle groups are her weakest. They share a unique symmetry, and it motivates Anne to have this side of herself brought out.

Despite this initial connection, the relationship quickly becomes toxic and abusive. Marie barks orders at Anne that are beyond what you'd hear from the toughest trainers, using hurtful insults as twisted motivational tactics. Moreover, Marie—on more than one occasion—physically injures Anne by pushing her past her limits, then guilt trips her for taking time off to recover.

But the pounds melt away, and the results are too good for Anne to cut ties. The compliments roll in, and her coveted beach body is indeed ready for summer. The hard work has paid off, and Marie still makes house calls when she's needed. After all, you can't argue with results.

When asked about New Year's resolutions, Osho says "all resolutions are imprisonments. You decide today for tomorrow? You have destroyed tomorrow." We reject certain versions of our tomorrow selves in the same way that we reject our today selves. Why slam the door on any of them? Christianity teaches the doctrine of "original sin," kicking us out of the garden for the unacceptable crime of being born. Last I checked, I didn't exactly have a say in the process. Wouldn't an all-loving god love all of me? Wouldn't unconditional love look like total acceptance of whichever you that you happen to be today, tomorrow, or yesterday? Some of you are probably shaking your heads, convinced that there are versions of yourself that you could never accept. If so, then that's fine… but I wonder if you could accept this version of yourself that doesn't accept the other versions. I'd start there. You might have more success finding acceptance in today than in another year.

> **Linus Van Pelt:** I never thought it was such a bad little tree. It's not bad at all, really. Maybe it just needs a little love.

A Charlie Brown Christmas (1965)

A2. White must win over black

As far as we can discern, the sole purpose of human existence is to kindle a light in the darkness of mere being.

— Carl Jung

Imagine a game that is 100% impossible to win. No matter how hard you practice or play, there's no chance of winning. Not today. Not tomorrow. Not ever. Moreover, even if you *somehow* managed to pull off the impossible and win at this game, you would immediately realize that it wasn't what you wanted after all. Does this sound like a game you want to play? If not, then I've got some bad news… Nearly *everybody* plays this game to the hilt for the majority of their lives. There's a very good chance that you're playing it as we speak. You've probably had lots of practice at it, and are basically a professional at it.

An improvement-oriented society positions stagnation as the enemy of progress. A government must show what they've done to advance their mandate through new legislation. A corporation must show their board of directors quarterly growth in its bottom line. An employee must show career advancement in order to be considered a professional success. Does this logic make any sense, though? Is stagnation objectively bad? Consider an employee stuck in a "dead-end job" who happens to love it and find it fulfilling. Are they a failure for settling for less than their potential, or are they living the dream that we all want? Maybe they enjoy the peace and quiet of living on a dead-end.

Most people walk around thinking that death is bad, despite wanting to die themselves. When I raise this idea, people tend to recoil and refute: "I don't want to die!" they confidently exclaim. However, a brief thought experiment reveals that living forever would obviously be a massive problem. Now their position shifts into "well I don't want to die right *now*." Another brief thought experiment reveals that when they die, it's going to be now. So is this now better than that now? That's not obvious to me. I wish I could have the same conviction as the refuters, but what do I know?

Someone can hold a belief like "I don't want to die" so strongly that it's as obvious to them as their name or age. Ask them the right questions, and they might be a minute away from dropping that obvious belief because they obviously don't believe it. Decades of deeply held belief can evaporate in an instant. They simply haven't thought it through, which begs the obvious question: What other deeply held beliefs of theirs might crumble upon the slightest investigation? Speaking for myself, it was pretty much all of them (though some of my beliefs required *very* deep digging to inspect thoroughly).

I first heard Alan Watts reference this particular game of black and white, noting that "once we get into the fear that black—the negative side—might win, we are compelled to play the game 'but white must win!' And from that start all our troubles." If this game is a fear response, then shouldn't we treat it with exposure therapy? In order to entertain this treatment, we must first pin down what it is we're actually afraid of when we play this game. What would black winning over white even look like? If this worst of worst case scenarios actually happened... then what? All of this is assuming that we have an illness requiring treatment in the first place. That's not obvious to me.

Story Time: The Trash Compounder

Inspired by the recent minimalist movement, you decide to declutter your small apartment. You round up all of the trash that no longer serves you, and toss it all down your building's garbage chute. All gone.

You return to your apartment to find bags of trash in the middle of your living space. You must have forgotten a few. You lug those over to the chute and dispose of them.

You return again to find even *more* garbage piled up inside your apartment than you bagged to begin with. Where's it all coming from? You can't live like this, so you drag it all over to the chute, which is now clogged. You leave it in the hall for the building to deal with.

You have to step over all of the bags to return to your apartment, where you're greeted at your doorway with a wall of trash preventing you from entering. Now you've got a full-blown crisis on your hands.

You toss enough bags into the hall to create some space to enter and sort out a plan of attack. You manage to step inside, but now the door won't close behind you, as there's a wall of garbage in the hall spilling in. You find yourself totally trapped in trash with no more moves available.

Defeated, you surrender to your surroundings, and things suddenly don't look so cluttered.

Allow me to clear up what this game looks like in some common examples I hear almost every day:

- Good must win over evil
- Love must win over hate
- Beauty must win over ugliness
- Peace must win over war
- Allies must win over enemies
- Life must win over death
- Health must win over illness
- Order must win over chaos
- Safety must win over danger
- Intelligence must win over ignorance
- Success must win over failure
- Justice must win over crime
- Winning must win over losing

I can hear you already: "Is this idiot advocating for evil, war, death, and crime?" The short answer is no. Of course not. That would make me a menace to society, and heroes must win over villains. But how do we operationalize that sentiment? Do we become the enemies of villains and go to war with them? Do we declare our hatred for them? Do we call them evil, ugly, or ignorant? Do we wish for their failure? Do we lock them up in a dangerous place and inflict illness upon them? Do we commit a crime and kill them? Wait... whose side are we on again?

In *The Dark Knight* (2008), the Joker sincerely confesses to Batman that "I don't wanna kill you! What would I do without you?" It seems like this villain isn't quite playing a game of "villains must win over heroes." On the other hand, our hero struggles to uphold his moral code of not killing the Joker when presented with several opportunities. As a vigilante playing a game of "justice must win over crime," Batman lives in constant conflict. Can you crime your way into justice? In *Batman Begins* (2005), a younger Batman lets his foe and former friend die despite clearly having the ability to save him. Are these the "right" or "wrong" moves? That's not obvious to me. But what do I know?

I know that you don't need to be a superhero or supervillain to recognize when you're playing this game. It can be as subtle as wanting to banish boredom from your life in favor of fun. Or perhaps you're seeking to stamp out a certain season, because "summer must win over winter." It can be as serious as a full-blown crusade or genocide to completely wipe out a whole class of people positioned as parasites. The next time you catch yourself playing any version of this game, consider the following question: Why so serious?

A3. This isn't a game

London is too full of fogs and serious people. Whether the fogs produce the serious people, or whether the serious people produce the fogs, I don't know.

— Oscar Wilde

One of the foundational aspects of Game A is the idea that it isn't a game at all. All of Game A's games are nestled within the "this isn't a game" game, which is what sets the stakes for everything we do. Life gets pretty serious when you believe it's not a game.

You've heard it all before:

- Life is short
- Life is precious
- Life is a gift
- You only live once
- Live life to the fullest
- Carpe diem
- Don't waste time
- Time is money
- Cherish the moment
- No regrets

The raising of the stakes seems to stem from an idea that life is a scarce resource that must not be wasted. If we looked at life as if it were a game, most of us would likely see it as one big championship match. We only get one shot, the clock is running down, and everything is on the line. So if life were a game, it would be the most serious game possible. What could be more serious than the most serious game? Easy: This isn't a game.

When said in the spirit of scarcity, these expressions look more like warnings than wisdom. Much like Ebenezer Scrooge in *A Christmas Carol* by Charles Dickens, we're haunted and told that we must live by some correct code. Don't waste your life, or else. This begs the obvious question: Or else what? If the stakes are so high, then surely there'd be some dire consequences implied. Much like many religious texts, Jacob Marley warns Scrooge that if he doesn't straighten up, then he faces an afterlife of eternal damnation bearing the weight of these heavy chains. While I concede that this punishment sounds unpleasant, it begs the next obvious question: Then what? I'm not convinced that the hypothetical afterlife chains sound heavier than the serious warnings about my present-day life, which I'm expected to lug around and pass on to the next generation.

I actually agree with most of the sayings about how life is short, precious, and a gift. However, I might say the same thing in the spirit of abundance, not scarcity. I would say "life is a gift" in the sense that it's all free. All of your time is bonus time; you couldn't waste it if you tried. Interestingly, youth recently popularized YOLO (you only live once) as a rather unserious expression justifying care-free behavior. The same generation also coined the term FOMO (fear of missing out), so perhaps they take their unseriousness very seriously.

We take life very seriously because we think we have to control the outcome of it. We tell ourselves that we have to accomplish this, or have that, or get there in order to be happy. We carry around these enormous expectations of what we need to do. Even when we're not doing the serious work required of the expectations, we're weighed down by the seriousness of not working on the work. We end up living with regret from the past, fear of the future, and disdain for the present.

Even when we recognize that we can't control the outcome, any perceived heightened stakes causes us to stress about that outcome we can't control. Bet $100 on a sports game, and you'll likely care a lot more about the outcome. It might be the perfect amount to inject some added tension and excitement to the experience of watching the game. Bet your life on the sports game, and it might get so serious that you can't bear to watch. You might die from the stress before it even ends. Suddenly, it's not so fun anymore.

Many of us even take our fun seriously. We plan out and try to optimize our leisure time in order to fulfill these expectations of our highest self. We feel pressure to perform at letting loose, because we don't want to waste our free time. How could you waste free time? It's free! How much did it cost you to be born? We commonly agree that life is a gift, and yet we act like we're terribly invested in it.

Amusement parks are supposed to be fun, yet some people still manage to make them miserable. Hospitals aren't supposed to be fun, yet some people still manage to make them a blast. According to Hunter Doherty "Patch" Adams, "laughter boosts the immune system and helps the body fight off disease, cancer cells, as well as viral, bacterial, and other infections." Maybe we should take our fun more seriously.

Story Time: First Steps

> Her first steps were met with applause and fanfare. All of the cameras in the room were rolling, and all eyes were on her. She hated what she was wearing, but everyone seemed to adore it.
>
> She started to get a little wobbly, and wasn't quite following the path laid out for her. She never liked being posed or forced to rehearse things, but got away with it because she was so cute.

She was getting tired of always performing on cue and under the pressure of everyone watching. She had been encouraged to just put one foot in front of the other. Easier said than done…

No longer able to support the weight, her legs finally gave out. Everyone was surprised to see that she found the whole thing hilarious, as she collapsed awkwardly to the ground with a grin.

She then stripped off her dress, and proceeded to make spitty sounds and funny faces at everyone, before turning her back and crawling away on all fours. The video would surely go viral.

Offstage, the designer watched in horror as the model made a mockery of his fashion show.

We feel the need to be "on" in social settings to project our best self, and have the chore of documenting it on social media. We manage to pile on more homework when we're not doing homework, then we wonder why we're stressed out. If we don't give ourselves a break during our break time, then when will we? People often go out and end up "chasing the night," always looking for fun like it's a precious resource to be mined. Then the night ends and they wonder why it sucked. They figure it must be because they didn't find any fun. As long as you're looking for fun, you won't have it. Trying to control the outcome of your evening is like trying to control the next hand you're dealt. Just play the cards you have and have fun!

If you've managed to find something that allows you to have fun, then please do me a favor and don't feel bad about enjoying it. Our whole notion of a "guilty pleasure" is patently absurd to me. Think about it… It's an indulgence so good that it must be bad… Isn't that just a pleasure? I understand that indulging in certain pleasures invites associated consequences, some of which might be less than desirable. However, if you're going to indulge in it, then why not enjoy it? Attaching a sense of guilt to it turns a win-lose into a lose-lose, inviting the negative consequence *and* robbing you of the enjoyment you should feel while indulging in the thing that you obviously enjoy. Either indulge and enjoy the indulging, or abstain and enjoy dodging the consequences of indulging. Now that I think about it, I wouldn't be surprised if Game A loves indulging in guilt itself, because it reinforces the "I'm not good enough" part of the story we tell ourselves.

How come when we indulge in watching a movie, we recognize that it isn't as serious as "real life"? When a man gets shot on the screen, it's less serious than when a man gets shot on our street. A game of monopoly doesn't seem as serious as a day of trading on the stock market. Are they really so different? I sell you an electric company for some paper money. You sell me a railroad for some paper money.

We seem to have disdain for the seriousness of the stakes, but fail to realize that they're entirely self-imposed. Betting your life on a sports game seems like an extreme example, but that line seems so arbitrarily drawn upon closer inspection. It's easy to see my life as being 100% at stake 100% of the time by virtue of being alive. To live at all is to risk death by definition. Can you feel the seriousness rising? I could argue that a child bets their life on every sports game they play. We would clearly see this as an inappropriately serious outlook. Maybe children feel the same way about our adult games.

We intuitively encourage children not to take games too seriously. We teach them "nobody likes a sore loser," "it's only a game," and "you'll get another chance to play again." My brother tells his son that "playing is winning." Why do we stop applying this wisdom to adult games? I guess it makes sense that we're unable to apply wisdom concerning games to things we perceive as non-games. Perhaps a best practice might be to always leave a little room for the possibility of viewing things as games... *especially* the "this isn't a game" game. That is a wonderful game, indeed. According to Alan Watts, "man suffers only because he takes seriously what the gods made for fun."

A4. Lost in the sauce

We don't see things as they are; we see them as we are.

— Anaïs Nin

This super serious world of ours places such a high priority on science, data, and facts that it leads to an overuse of the logical left brain. This bias is built into the primary way we transfer knowledge: Language. Our very understanding of understanding itself is made up of linguistic building blocks, whether that language is English, math, chemistry, or computer code. We even teach the arts with a heavy focus on the language of logic, neglecting the right brain language of creativity. Moreover, we seem to *completely* forget about the right brain language of non-language. I learned all of what I consider to be my deepest understanding of the world in the non-language of experience. I'm afraid it wouldn't package well into a PowerPoint presentation.

Our minds are constantly overloaded with information packaged in the language of concepts. We view everything through this word salad prism, and it all just feels so... saucy. We can't help but drench everything we encounter with a heaping helping of sauce. I'll listen to people talk about their nuanced understanding of nutrition, nonpartisanship, or numerology and ask myself: "What are we talking about?" No wonder kids look at us sideways. We're so bogged down in sauce that we can't see the meat hidden beneath it. A hot dog is better with a little sauce, in exactly the way that a little left brain introduction or build up can improve the right brain experience. But a hot dog with a whole container of mustard is disgusting. You no longer taste the hotdog, or even the mustard for that matter.

Labels are a disaster. They're an extremely practical tool that we can thank language for. However, they're *so* practical that an overreliance upon this shortcut leads us away from the intended destination, and toward more shortcuts to shortcuts… Then we end up on a longcut to nowhere. A label is supposed to point at the thing it's labeling, acting as a sort of short-hand or stand-in for it to facilitate communication. However, when we forget to actually attach the label to the thing we're labeling, then we confuse the label for the thing itself. Now we're pointlessly using labels to point *away* from the thing we think we're using them to point at. Too much signage is bad for navigating.

We teach kids that "this is a coffee cup," but how does "coffee cup" in any way reflect its nature? Instead we should teach kids that "we *call* this a coffee cup." I could write a 10,000 word dissertation on what a coffee cup is, but it would amount to 100% sauce; the words could never stand in for the thing they're describing. You cannot feel the warmth of "coffee cup" in your hands, smell the contents of "coffee cup," or drink from "coffee cup." At the end of the day, what we're really talking about is [ting ting ting, ssshhhshhsspp, ahhhh]... This would be much easier to demonstrate in person, as we're running into the limitations of language.

Watch a toddler point at an animal or vehicle and mimic the sound it makes. *That* is how labels should be used. In fact, many ancient languages call animals by the sounds they make. This seems rather intuitive to me. After all, "moo" is a more accurate descriptor of that four-legged thing than "cow," and "vroom" is a more accurate descriptor of that four-wheeled thing than "car."

Exercise: What is it?

Pick up a common household object.

a) What is it?

b) Write the first three words that come to mind to describe it.

c) Examine it closer, and write another 10 words to describe it.

d) Write down 10 words that it ISN'T.

e) Write down five words that it was in a prior state and five that it could be in a future state.

f) Do a quick sketch of it.

g) Write down 10 words to describe your drawing of it.

h) Revisit and reconsider (a)

Language is great for things like "pass the salt," but is a disaster for things like "I am a person." You say "pass the salt," then I hand you the thing you were after. Done. Not that saucy. The word "salt," in this example, is standing in for a finger pointing at the thing we call "salt." We aren't really talking about the concept of "salt." It's self-evident that you want that white stuff on your food. We aren't bogged down in language because we drop it as soon as the salt is passed.

When I say "I am a person," it might sound just as simple and pragmatic as "pass the salt," but it's only hard to see the sauce here because there's so much of it. While we could say that "I" is simply pointing at yourself in the way that "salt" is pointing at the thing on the table, is that really how we use it? If I asked a thousand people to explain the concept of "I" in twenty words, I'd probably receive a thousand distinct and saucy explanations. On the other hand, you'd probably struggle to fill the twenty words explaining the "salt" that is passed. I suspect this is because we don't carry around a bunch of stories about "salt."

We carry around archives upon archives of stories about "I." It has hopes and dreams, a history and a future, a body and a soul, and is even a key player in "pass the salt" despite not even being mentioned. I'm not definitively saying that "salt" doesn't have hopes and dreams, because it might. I'm saying that we don't engage with "salt" on that complex and nuanced conceptual level. You probably wouldn't tell your life story to an interviewer with a flippant grunt (though it would be pretty epic if you did). Things are already getting saucy, and we're still on the concept of "I." Examining what is meant by "am" would likely invite a whole other tsunami of sauce upon us.

Imagine how much sauce has been dispensed in this book already. Each page is completely covered in it, but that hasn't stopped you from eating it up. We're slaves to the siren song of sauce. Like the ringwraiths in J. R. R. Tolkien's *The Lord of the Rings*, our overreliance upon language has made us dependent upon it for our meaning making. It's no longer just a tool in our belt. It's the idol we worship by never letting go of it. If I left the next page blank, your mind would likely fill it in with sauce. So we've taken the language tool from our belt, used language to deify it, and then used language to worship our language idol. Saucy. We made language, now language makes us. But if our meaning is now made of language, then what was it made of before?

Do we recognize the inadequacies of language? In *Birdman or (The Unexpected Virtue of Ignorance)* (2014), a theater critic has a flower held up to her face and is pointedly asked: "Do you even know what that is?" Michael Keaton's character accuses her of being lazy, explaining that "you can't see this thing if you don't know how to label it. You mistake all those little noises in your head for true knowledge." She never even looks at the flower, waits for him to finish, then replies by labeling him and leaves. He tried to tell her that she's lost in the sauce. I guess she missed his point.

You would likely recognize the inadequacy of a bucket full of holes when it comes to holding water. Try using language to capture an experience and tell me it isn't a similar exercise in futility. I'm not saying language is totally useless. A leaky bucket can still hold water. A poem can still elicit a memory or a feeling of an experience. However, no collection of words describing "wetness" will elicit the feeling you have when I push you into a lake.

Many of us have had brushes with non-Game A experiences in the past, but we tend to label them from our sauce-centered perspective as being "checked out," "spaced out," or "out of it." Out of what, exactly? In those less saucy moments, you're clearly not playing the improvement, label, judgment, or doing game. Notice the negative connotation of those labels, as we seem to equate "out of it" with being out of life itself. Yet when you stare at the clouds and are "out of it," you aren't out of awareness or out of life at all. You arguably couldn't possibly be any closer to them than that. Jiddu Krishnamurti would describe such an experience as choiceless or complete awareness, which can only take place when one is no longer aware of "awareness."

Story Time: The Unsipped Beers

Taylor and Alex love a cold beer, and meet at a pub every Friday night to enjoy one. This Friday, they order the new seasonal ale, and take their first sips with a keen focus on how they might describe what they're tasting. What proceeds is an hour-long debate over whether the beer is sweet or savory, while their nearly full glasses warm on the table untouched.

I'm a big fan of YouTube, as it seems to be more engaging and community-oriented than other social media platforms built around purely passive consumption. It can be easy to mistake highly engaged social media use as a substitute for real social interaction. I'm not saying that social media is 100% fake. I'm saying that the number of likes on your post can't help you move your couch. For every minute of golf instructional videos you watch, you would ideally be hitting balls for an hour. Otherwise, you're not playing golf. You're playing at playing golf, which is a totally different game. That game is fine and has its own value, but you can quickly fall into the trap of becoming an expert in swing direction and swing path having never actually swung a club. Engage with the thing itself, not the thing standing in for the thing you think you're engaged in.

I've recently developed a renewed fondness for Plato's "Allegory of the Cave," found in Book VII of *The Republic*. From my perspective, it paints a picture that so accurately depicts ringwraiths drowning in sauce that it's scary. The intense irony I see is that a ringwraith reads the image believing that "knowledge" is the truth that they've found outside of the cave of ignorance, whereas I see them as chained up in the cave of "outside the cave" and describing the shadows of "knowledge" projected on the wall. I bet many philosophy experts are convinced that I've completely misinterpreted the allegory. Maybe they can show me the light.

You can't sauce your way out of sauce. My understanding of the Socratic method is simply holding up a mirror until the speaker eventually sees how saucy their own sauce is. It's super effective! So if we're all hopeless ringwraiths drowning in some sauce cave, then it begs the obvious question: How does one escape? You probably won't like my answer, but I swear this is the method: One simply does.

A5. The habit (I can do things)

When life gives you lemons, don't make lemonade. Make life take the lemons back! Get mad! I don't want your damn lemons. What the hell am I supposed to do with these? Demand to see life's manager!

— Cave Johnson (Portal 2)

Someone playing Game A interprets every message—especially one about spiritual guidance—as a call to action. You can tell them that from a Game B point of view, action doesn't exist, but they'll hear those words as another call to action, and start trying to solve the riddle. The trick to showing them the passive Game B perspective is to take this doing-oriented bias and turn it around on them with another call to action: Please demonstrate your ability to interfere with this process. If you were truly in control of your actions, surely you could control whether or not you do them in the first place. You could show me that you could do *nothing at all*. What would that look like?

Let's say tomorrow you try your hardest to do nothing at all. Maybe you decide you're going to lay in bed all day to prove your agency. If I showed a hundred random strangers a live video feed of you demonstrating your non-action and asked them what you were doing, how many of them would say you're doing "nothing at all"? How many would say you're "lying in bed" or "sleeping"? Have you really shown anyone that you're capable of inaction? Even if 100% of those strangers agreed that you're doing "nothing at all," then aren't you guilty of the action of proving your agency? That doesn't sound like nothing to me.

I'll go as far as to concede that by staying in bed all day, you're demonstrating your ability to do nothing at all by virtue of your belief that you're doing nothing at all. Things get interesting if we see how far we can push this. Could you do nothing at all for a week? A month? Even during that day, how long can you stay in bed until you need to eat, use the bathroom, or stretch your legs? Even if we draw a bigger circle around these apparent actions and define them as non-actions, how far can we push those? How much can you eat until you run out of food and have to go grocery shopping? How many days can you stay in bed before you have to go to work or school? Despite your best efforts to do nothing at all, you'll find yourself completing tasks that appear fairly active in nature. If you found yourself running to catch a bus, would you still believe that you were doing nothing at all?

I see a strong argument that you're actually *so* active that you're utterly incapable of inaction. But if you can't not do, then are you really at the wheel at all? Again: Please demonstrate your ability to interfere with this process. If everything you do is your doing, then what happens to you is a product of your doing. Said another way: What happens to you *is* your doing. Alan Watts explains that this was the meaning of "karma" before it got twisted into some cosmic force of justice.

How do you distinguish the things you've done from the things that happen to you? Would you prefer some choice in your choicelessness or some choicelessness in your choice? It's six in one hand, half a dozen in the other. Even Dr. Manhattan, the god-like character who sees his past, present, and future simultaneously in Alan Moore's *Watchmen* (1986), can't seem to tell the difference: "A world grows up around me. Am I shaping it, or do its predetermined contours guide my hand?"

Exercise: Budget Cuts

The cost of food in your town has drastically increased over the past few months. In an effort to budget accordingly, you stop getting haircuts indefinitely.

a) Your friends notice that you started "growing your hair out," but this doesn't feel entirely accurate to you. How might you clarify your intent?

b) If you feel the cost of food is high due to the government's trade policies, would it be fair to say that government officials are growing your hair out?

c) Two years into this budgeting practice, your hair reaches its terminal length. Who's responsible for its lack of growth?

d) If the state of your hair was just a byproduct of your circumstances, could you say the same about the state of your mind? Did you choose your answers, or is the author of the questions responsible for them?

Much like this idea of "growing your hair," we have a tendency to actionify things that seem entirely passive upon closer inspection. For example, it's common practice for active individuals to use their smartphones to track various metrics of their performance in fitness and recovery. One of the most absurd metrics tracked is "sleep performance," as if you were 100% on and "doing" the task of sleeping. Someone might pull up their smartphone app and tell themselves that "I only scored a 70% on my sleep performance, so I'll have to do better tonight." How does one "do better" at something as passive as sleeping? It doesn't get much more passive than that. You might as well be mad at yourself when the weather turns miserable. If we simply changed the language in the app from "sleep performance" to "quality of sleep," we could avoid this trap of burdening people with the expectation of non-stop doing.

Think of a song. Just do it. Got one? Excellent choice. You probably feel like that choice was voluntary or under your control. However, if you think it through a little, you might find that the water gets murkier. Do you have control over your musical preferences, over the set of all songs that you remember, or over the options that popped into your head when prompted? Even at the moment of selection, how did you decide that you had decided? Did you "choose" the song first and then it felt right, or did the song feel right and then you "chose" it? If you didn't choose a song at all, were you conditioned not to by my annoying prompts? I wouldn't blame you, and wouldn't have a choice in not blaming you. Okay, that was annoying. I didn't have a choice!

A6. The blue pill

Disneyland is presented as imaginary in order to make us believe that the rest is real.

— Jean Baudrillard

> **DISCLAIMER**
>
> I use the **blue pill** and **red pill** motifs from *The Matrix* to help advance my points about conditioning. I feel like the trope is widely understood and fits well with the picture I wish to paint for maximum clarity. I'm not inferring any other connotation with the terms, which have been adopted by various political and cultural movements.

This section examines the culture of Game A. More specifically, it digs down into conditioning running so deep that it may be clouding you from even considering an alternative perspective.

One of the things I think Game A gets right is a tendency to cling to artifacts of importance. We cherish sentimental items and pass them on for generations. I find myself clinging to this aspect of materialism as a source of deep meaning, and see many upsides to the practice. However, Game A tends to also cling to many artifacts of unimportance, causing the important things to get buried under the clutter. So much of the physical and emotional baggage we carry around doesn't serve us in the way that a beloved family heirloom or story does. It's easy to see how identifying with Game A pillars can quickly bog you down in a tangled web of conflicting rules and rituals.

We tell ourselves these stories, constantly reinforcing the narratives of our lives. Maybe you tell yourself a version of the "woe is me" story, always justifying why you don't deserve for things to work out. Maybe you hold yourself to impossible standards, always ranking yourself behind the other perfect people on social media. Despite the obvious negative connotations of such stories, they do provide a genuine level of comfort and reassurance to those repeating them.

There's a sense of belonging to be found in a story like "my place may be no good, but it's good to be in my place." Misery loves company. Looping on these stories confirms the bias established by them in the first place, feeding a spiral in which it seems truer and truer with each repetition. It's a lot like working out. We put in so many reps over so many years that the muscle memory becomes strong. Old habits die hard. Do we repeat these stories because they're true, or are they true because we repeat them?

Each story is like a pacifier for a toddler who has outgrown it, but can't let it go. While the stories may be soothing, they're ultimately holding you back from the benefits of moving on. When my nephew had outgrown his pacifier, you could tell he really wanted the benefits of being a big boy, but didn't want to lose the benefit of the pacifier. But how do you move on without moving on? You can't hold on into letting go. We realized that what he was really wrestling with was heartache, and what he needed was closure. The solution was for him to wave and say goodbye to his pacifier, giving it a loving sendoff. You only cling to it because it's familiar. You haven't stopped to investigate whether it sucks or not. It's always easier to take one more suck on the existential pacifier than to break a habit that sucks.

Culture runs so much deeper than people realize. Your thoughts are biased in structure and substance by the languages they're formed in. Someone else taught you that language. Someone else taught you that you can think. Someone else taught you that you are you. I repeat: The entire notion that you are you was someone else's idea. You had to be conditioned to be you before you started pinning other conditioned attributes and stories to that now overloaded corkboard. If the corkboard is holding up all of the tangled aspects of your identity, then what's holding up the corkboard? Were you you before you were you?

We have a term for anyone whose identity corkboard closely matches the corkboard of the culture they were raised in: Normal. You could say one of the character traits of normal people is cultural consistency, since most of their character traits are culturally consistent. They tend to operate largely within the box they were given, and tend to be easy to predict. Their opinions, beliefs, and feelings about any given topic will likely align closely with what you'd expect from that culture. Interestingly, the very culturally consistent tend not to be very logically consistent, often flip-flopping into seemingly contradictory positions in order to mimic whatever the popular dance of the day is. They don't care what's for dinner. They just want a seat at the table.

Once we've all got our seats at the table, the question arises as to what's being served for dinner and by whom. My advertising professor in university—shoutout to Dr. Strangelove—would refer to "the broccoli argument," which proposes that consumers will consume whatever is in front of us. The basic idea is that if a child is adamant that they don't like broccoli, then all you have to do is keep putting broccoli in front of them every day for dinner. They'll eventually eat it (and like it too). Even if they don't eat it and continue to hate it, then broccoli is still at the forefront of their mind. They're probably not thinking about cauliflower (but I bet you just did for the same reason). The mainstream media controls the narrative by controlling what's served on the plate. The basic fact of the exposure, irrespective of the particular messaging, has a conditioning effect over a prolonged period.

It's difficult to think of anything that conditions us more through exposure than advertising. Most of us dislike advertising and are convinced it doesn't have any effect on us. Would corporations spend millions of dollars on it if it didn't generate sales? Something tells me they aren't in it for the artform. Your wallet may be able to dodge most of the sales pitches you encounter, but your mind may be quietly eating them up in the background without your consent. How many before-and-after photos do you have to be exposed to until you start to think about yourself in those terms? As long as we're constantly bombarded with "be better" broccoli, our minds become boxed into the thought patterns that make the next "be better" broccoli we encounter look more appealing. We recognize that we're being sold the lotion that will soothe our itch. We don't recognize that we're also being sold the notion that we have an itch in the first place.

One of the compulsions that we're locked into from an early age is what I call "boxing." I'm not talking about stepping into a ring and throwing some punches (which would actually make a great remedy for the compulsion in question). I'm talking about a mental process of constantly packaging, labeling, and filing sensory experiences away into their designated and delineated conceptual categories. Think of it as the mental equivalent of that baby toy with the uniquely shaped blocks that we're supposed to push through the corresponding holes. Language is *fantastic* at this, to the point that it becomes problematic when you want to experience the sensory input without the associated urge to clean up the mess.

This habit of making knee-jerk value judgments can be extremely difficult to turn off. Why can't something just be what it is? It has to be labeled as x, y, or z and filed away in our language library before we can even begin to interact with it. But at that point, we can't even begin to interact with it because we just filed it away. Then we begin to package and file away that perceived interaction, which never really took place outside of the library.

Think of the boxer as a diligent librarian, and of vocabulary as their Dewey Decimal system. It can be an uncomfortable feeling when books aren't filed away in their proper place on their proper shelf. Sound familiar? If not, then I better speak for myself. Maybe my morning coffee is good, that dog is cute, I like that social media post, that driver is a jerk, my lunch was tasty, that class was boring, etc. Some mornings, I'll take the first sip of a coffee and file it away as "good," then proceed to file each subsequent sip into the "good" box. I've already determined that the coffee is good. Why can't I just enjoy it?

It's bad enough that the boxer can't experience anything without making these snap judgments. What's worse is that they're more than happy to use someone else's prefabricated and prelabeled box, which may or may not be a great match in shape, size, or title for the experience being boxed. This potential inconsistency between sensory input and perceived experience is not a problem for the boxer, whose primary concern is that everything be boxed.

I need to be told by the critic that the movie is good before I see it. I need to be told by the sommelier that the wine is fruity before I taste it. Are we so afraid of saying that the coffee is smooth to us when the label on the pot says "bold"? It's almost like individual taste is a matter of individual taste. In "Birds with Broken Wings," Ben Caplan sings that "I want the trees in single file," my "metaphors unraveled," and my "poetry defined." We teach our kids poetry as defined with a "correct" interpretation, then we're surprised when they're locked up and afraid to express themselves. After all, they might say something that doesn't fit into our inherited prefabricated and prelabeled boxes.

Various aspects of Game A cause people to become locked up. Lack of self confidence has an obvious stifling and shrinking effect. Morality and responsibility apply constant pressure to do the right thing and take things seriously. Information overload monopolizes our attention and puts us into a passive frame of receiving. The burden of long to-do lists burns us out and seizes up our ability to act. All of this adds up to a sort of analysis paralysis that becomes our conditioned normal state.

It's normal for us to want to be normal. I encourage you to look up the Asch conformity experiments, which show how it's more important for most of us to be in the in-group than to be right. We'll deny our own senses, effectively lying to ourselves and others, if it means we get that coveted seat at the table. The game of musical chairs is a wonderful example of how we train these habits and motives into ourselves through culture. Fifty years later, the same kid wants to be on the board of directors of a company that they don't even like and can't figure out why. This is an interesting form of boxing, in that we box *ourselves* into categories and communities at the expense of our individuality.

There are excellent social, tribal, and evolutionary explanations for this boxing habit. If we didn't make snap judgments of others, we'd expose ourselves to danger and deny ourselves attraction. If we dissolved our desire to fit in, we'd also dissolve our support networks. If we savored the nuance of every blade of grass we walked past, we'd never make it to our destination. These are perfectly practical shortcuts to take, but I worry that we take them so often that we've lost sight of the scenic route. I'm concerned that boxing is *so* harmless and intuitive that it goes unchecked and unnoticed. Constant boxing makes it harder to dive into deeper conversations, to get stuck into sticky problems, or to get swept up in moving art. If you simply read the card next to the painting and repeat "nice Picasso" or "this is cubism," then you're more engaged with the explanatory card than the painting itself. To box an experience is to block an experience.

Game A summary

Now that we've established the main pillars defining Game A, you might start to recognize them in the actions and beliefs of others. You might meet a Christian who believes that they must repent for their sin (I'm not good enough and I must improve), that God must triumph over Satan (white must win over black), and that their literal salvation is at stake (this isn't a game). You might meet a yogi whose self worth is tied up in mastering the next pose (I'm not good enough and I must improve), who wants to eliminate all stress from their life (white must win over black), and who plants trees because it's the responsible thing to do (this isn't a game). While they appear in many different forms, those first three pillars are the easiest to recognize and are the driving force behind pretty much everyone's life. Find someone motivated by other pursuits and you have met a rare soul indeed.

I'm sure many will read this book as a rebuke of Game A, so I feel compelled to highlight some of its strengths. It provides purpose and meaning to its players, and the fact that nearly everyone is a player means it provides *shared* purpose and meaning in the form of culture. Whether or not that culture is one worth pursuing is debatable. Having unattainable goals baked in makes it very well adapted to survival. It keeps you playing, like a slot machine that gives you the odd feeling of winning without ever paying out a big jackpot. No matter what happens, you can always blame "yourself" for not "trying hard enough" and spin again. That way, no one ever stops to think that "maybe this thing isn't working because this thing doesn't actually work." Slot machines are fun to play every now and then, and when low stakes are involved. But when you're playing 24/7 and the stakes are so high that it no longer becomes a game, then it's probably not a winning strategy.

Game A is amazing at a lot of things, but it's terrible at achieving the ultimate improvement goal of Game A. If things are so bad, then let's change them already. We fight wars in the pursuit of stability. Jiddu Krishnamurti says "there have been, during the last five thousand years, nearly five thousand wars. Is that stability?" It's like trying to reach the top floor of a building by running laps around the lobby. It's a method so useless that it's actually an obstacle in the way of achieving the aim. Just take the elevator.

Game B

Illustration by Austin Beaton

What is Game B?

Game B is the game we play before we learn Game A, and what presents itself as an alternative when we drop Game A.

I've listed below what I feel are the six pillars of Game B, which will be explored in this section. I've tried to make them as clear as possible, but I've also left some sections intentionally nebulous. Game B is *much* harder to define than Game A, so I'd rather not try to bottle it too precisely. My goal is to paint a loose picture that gives you the general feeling of Game B. Think of it like an impressionist painting, and meet it in the middle with your own interpretation.

Game B pillars:

1. Full expression
2. Yin yang
3. What a ride/show
4. Smelling the roses
5. The weather
6. The red pill

In stark contrast with Game A's active focus, Game B language tends to be much more passive. Someone who fell down this rabbit hole might describe witnessing how things are happening, instead of doing or accomplishing things. They might report having an out-of-body experience, losing their sense of agency, or a new-found belief in fate. They might start expanding their definition of themselves, feeling like "a part of a whole," "connected to something bigger," or like "an extension of the universe." In broader terms, Game B language can sound pretty woo woo from a Game A perspective.

The unconventional nature of Game B makes it difficult to point to any popular icons as potential ambassadors, since most popular people tend to be popular for Game A reasons. Artists, outcasts, gurus, and people who see the world differently than most seem to offer the best examples. They tend to operate along the fringes of society, and those who break into the mainstream are known *because* of their eccentricities. Some notable exceptions include world renowned scientists known for Game A reasons, but who cleverly package Game B insights into more conventional wisdom. I'm only writing this book to Trojan Horse my message into a Game A package. The very young and the very old also offer excellent entry points into Game B insights.

Game B gods:

- The Joker
- Tom Waits
- Paul Klee
- Vincent Van Gogh
- Pablo Picasso
- Salvador Dalí
- Alan Watts
- Jiddu Krishnamurti
- Osho
- Lao Tzu
- Zen masters
- Winnie-the-Pooh
- Forrest Gump
- Mr. Rogers
- Socrates
- Aldous Huxley
- Henry David Thoreau
- Carl Sagan
- Richard Feynman
- Terence McKenna
- Rupert Sheldrake
- Jill Bolte Taylor
- The old and wise
- The imminently dying
- Babies and children (toddlers especially)

Watch any toddler, and you'll notice that they're motivated by *very* different things than your average adult. It's not because they're less sophisticated versions of adults. It's because they're playing an entirely different game. The same can be said for some older people, who become more child-like in their actions and demeanor once they finally give up on Game A.

This other game appears to be the "source code" that we're all born playing before we unlearn it. Toddlers are particularly interesting to watch because you can often see the stark contrast between both games, as they've got one foot in each. They might simultaneously be frustrated as they struggle to improve at a new skill with their hands, and be mesmerized by the fact that they've got hands at all.

Unlike Game A's drowning in a sea of saucy words, Game B language is… it's more like… wait… I can't seem to find the right… (it sounds a lot like this). That is, language can often break down altogether, as words utterly fail to capture an intended meaning, feeling, or experience. Non-verbal communication might rise to the surface, as words fall off a cliff. Someone might have trouble forming sentences, or struggle with spelling and grammar, as if they were unlearning language. Personally, seeing the Game B side of things dramatically changed my relationship with language. I became much less interested in using it "properly," and started using it more playfully. I was just struggling to write a sentence that was here, which I deleted after taking a refreshing pee break. Ahhhhh… Where was I?

Whereas Game A language strives for improvement, Game B sounds more like deep acceptance. It tends to be more grounded in the present, which Game A rejects in favor of a better tomorrow. This acceptance can not only sound like profound contentment or fulfillment, but also like deep sadness or suffering. Whereas Game A seeks to spin out of the darkness, Game B might go deeper into it, either out of curiosity or an understanding that darker darks make for lighter lights. That's not to say that Game B necessarily welcomes pain and misery, but it certainly sees the value in it. It views life's tragedies as worthy of experiencing in the same way a tragic movie, play, or book is worth the price of admission when it moves you to tears. From a Game B point of view, you're always getting maximum juice for your squeeze, no matter what that looks like. Things are as they are, and couldn't possibly be better.

B1. Full expression

I like you just the way you are.

— Mr. Rogers

If you begin to drop Game A, then the natural pillar that replaces "I'm not good enough and I must improve" is "I *am* good enough and I couldn't improve if I tried." That may sound like a radical belief to you. Let's examine what that looks like in practice.

We previously covered the ubiquity of before-and-after photos in advertising as a means of resonating with the Game A perspective. This format is entirely based on the assumption that the "after" person is an improved version of the "before" person. Notice how silly this format looks if you start seeing everyone as perfect the way they are: Perfect person on the left... Perfect person on the right... Why do I need this product? I look at someone who sees themselves as entirely not good enough, and I see them as entirely good enough as they are.

Is an oak tree an improved version of an acorn? Why should a child feel compelled to improve as they age? Is a flower that doesn't bloom a failed flower? Why should someone with a failed business be a failed person? Is there an optimal length for a blade of grass? Why should there be an optimal length for our hair? From a Game B perspective, humans grow in the exact same way that plants grow, instead of growing in terms of improvement.

Story Time: The Three Masters

Joe has never done yoga, has back pain, and can't touch his toes. He spends most of his time on the couch and considers himself a TV trivia buff, watching anything and everything he can.

Ken maintains a moderate yoga routine. He is able to get into most intermediate postures, and even some advanced ones. He watches some TV, mainly sticking to his favorite dramas, and even some guilty pleasures.

Max doesn't own a TV and will never see any of the great shows of our time. He devotes nearly all of his time to yoga, and is able to realize the "full expression" of even the most advanced postures.

Is Joe's life a tragic tale of the life not lived? Are Ken's habits a good example for those seeking a healthy work-life balance to follow? Is Max someone we should make a statue of, to honor and recognize his achievements? What if all three of these men have realized the "full expression" of the postures of their lives?

A common way that people try to improve the world is by spreading love. Seems reasonable enough. I love love. But is love the best? That's not obvious to me. A love-obsessed culture puts love up on a pedestal and upholds it as the gold standard that all other feelings should live up to. Seeing full expression levels the playing field by elevating all feelings onto the pedestal with love. There's plenty of space up there for anger, jealousy, understanding, and confusion. As Jimi Hendrix sings, "they're all bold as love."

As much as I love love, I also love me some good anguish. As a poker player, I'm always chasing the feeling that comes when I'm faced with a difficult decision. My opponent barrels into me with a big bet, and all I can beat is a bluff. I'm rewinding and playing over the hand in my head, considering bet sizes, and reading their current body language. Are they bluffing? Why would they bluff in this spot?? Would they bet that much if they were bluffing??? Are they trying to make it look bluffy to induce me to call???? They just reached for their drink twice in the same minute. Are they nervous????? What does it mean?????? It's utterly agonizing... and it's the best.

What about genuine anguish outside of a silly poker game? How could that be as desirable as love? Full expression isn't so much about seeing everything as the "best," but more about seeing it all as the most "it" that it can be. 10/10 anguish is a *very* different feeling than 10/10 love, but full expression recognizes that both knobs dial up to a ten. Moreover, full expression sees 4/10 anguish as 10/10 at being 4/10 anguish, if that makes sense.

Let's pretend there's a knob labeled "now experience" in your consciousness. If we cranked it to maximum and it got stuck in this position, what effect might that produce? This can be difficult to imagine when your now experience is particularly uneventful, but it will blow your mind if you see what I mean. Listen for a moment and see if you hear anything.

If you didn't hear anything, then you just got the maximum "didn't hear anything" experience. Rock on. You're always exactly where you're supposed to be. The only thing you need to be is what you are. Good luck being anything other than what you are, or being anywhere other than where you are. You can't be anything but yourself, because even if you think you aren't being yourself, then that is you being the fraud version of yourself. You might as well be yourself, because you already are to the fullest possible extent. There's nowhere to go and nothing to do. You're the full expression of you. The crowd goes wild.

Seeing full expression is like having a teacher tell you that you never need to do homework ever again. Suddenly, the world is one big extracurricular playground. If you feel weighed down by the constant pressure to perform, then full expression makes that weight as light as a feather. It's the realization that no matter what you do, a metaphorical line of judges will always hold up signs showing 10/10 across the board. You woke up this morning? Tens. You forgot to take out the trash? Tens. You're reading this book? Tens. You XYZ LMNOP'd? Tens. The judges can only ever hold up ten, because it's the only numbered card in front of them. You continue to stick every landing. Bravo! Encore!

One of the things I love about Game B is that it makes me feel like I'm on my own hero's journey. I feel like Hercules acting out his fate with no script to follow. No matter what I "do," I'm fulfilling my intended purpose. It's ironic that Game B makes me feel this way, when Game A uses the archetype of the hero's journey as a call to action. Culturally, parents teach their kids that if they want to be like Luke Skywalker from the *Star Wars* saga, then they need to act like a Jedi. From my perspective, they already are the chosen one; they can't not be.

You might be reading this and thinking that I'm advocating for the shirking of all responsibility. Full expression doesn't mean that if you're a student, then you suddenly can pass all your courses without doing any homework. It's more of a perspective shift. It's seeing that doing a chore is what living your best life looks like, rather than doing a chore in order to live your best life. You don't need to do anything in order to live your best life. You're living your best life no matter what you do. From this lens, everything starts to look like a game for the sake of itself. The homework isn't some necessary task in order to achieve the tens from the judges when you graduate. It isn't a means to an end. It's a perfectly worthy end in and of itself.

Seeing this perspective doesn't necessarily make unpleasant things any less unpleasant, but it does bring a level of deep acceptance and borderline celebration of unpleasant things. You aren't resisting the unpleasantness of it, because those judges are still showing you tens. Even if the thing is 10/10 unpleasant, then sitting in that unpleasantness feels like the 10/10 place to be. It's like receiving constant feedback that "this is okay," even when it might not intuitively feel okay at all.

If the best version of yourself is stuck doing homework, then this must be the best game in town right now. You must want to be doing it on some deep level, even if it's just to feel how unpleasant it is. If you're wondering what value there could possibly be in feeling something unpleasant, then it might be time for a lesson in yin yang 101.

B2. Yin yang

There is a crack, a crack in everything
That's how the light gets in

— Leonard Cohen (Anthem)

Are pleasant games the only games worth playing? It's obvious why a child wants to go to the playground to play the sandbox game or the swing game. It's less obvious why we might want to get dumped in order to play the heartbreak game. It's easy for us to say things like "the lower your lows, the higher your highs," but it doesn't make the "I'm at rock bottom" game a sudden joy to play. This section will examine how the entire strength of the unpleasant game is in its unpleasantness. Why would we want that? We don't, and that's the whole point.

We're constantly bombarded with "white must win over black" messaging from politicians, who promise things like progress over regress, order over chaos, and justice over lawlessness. I'm not saying that we should throw out all of our laws. That would be flipping to "black must win over white," which is effectively the same position said another way. I'm saying that we can't have justice without lawlessness. If everybody followed the rules, then we wouldn't need to enforce them. There'd be no need for the concept of justice, or even for the rules themselves.

A toddler needs to break the rules in order to find out where the boundaries are. A society is no different. Most of us agree that we need to keep updating our laws. How could we do this if our laws were never challenged? We can't have good examples of citizens without bad examples. The reason we don't break the rules is because we see the consequences for those who do. Thank goodness we have them to show us the way. To say that "justice must prevail" makes for a great soundbite, but is philosophically bankrupt upon closer inspection. I can't understand why we don't have a philosophy minister and shadow minister to dig beneath this surface-level messaging. The politician says "peace must win over war," but now we're waging a war on war. So much for peace. If we were truly advocating for peace, wouldn't we want to make peace with war?

Is it even possible to have peace without war or rules without rule breakers? This may sound like a bunch of hypothetical semantic nonsense, but hear me out. Try to explain the concept of "off" without ever referring to "on." Can you point to something that is objectively big? Big compared to what? Big implies small, on implies off, and black implies white. They go together, as two sides of the same coin. Show me a buy that isn't also a sale.

Exercise: The Edge of Space

Imagine a universe consisting only of solid matter. There isn't an ounce of space in this universe. It's solid all the way through. Does it have an edge?

Imagine another universe consisting entirely of space. This universe is a completely empty void. No matter where you look, there's nothing but space… Space between what?

During the time when I was having daily profound revelations about yin yang, I had this idea that the sidewalk I walked on was constantly threatening "not sidewalk." We think of the sidewalk as this solid and permanent thing, but I can't help but see the potential for it to flip at any moment, in the way that day is always threatening night. Most of us have experienced a day that was going perfectly smoothly, and then turned on a dime into something wildly different. The seed of chaos is always lurking in order and ready to bloom. The Titanic was drastically short on lifeboats because it was believed to be unsinkable.

We say we want to avoid tragedies, and yet we hold onto them as some of our most compelling and widely shared stories. We agree that Vincent Van Gogh led a largely tragic life, but we love to tell his story and admire his paintings. Those paintings we love are a product of his tragic life, so shouldn't we love that too? They go together. No Van Gogh, no paintings. As Thich Nhat Hanh says: "No mud, no lotus." Whenever I'm having a particularly bad week, I like to think of it as paying a yin yang tax. If all of your days were good days, they wouldn't be good days. They'd just be days.

The only way we recognize a Van Gogh painting as a Van Gogh is in contrast with a Monet or a Gaugain. If you change the things that don't make you what you are, then you change the things that make you what you are (both are equally shaping you). If you grew up poor and revised your past to remove all notion of wealth, then did you grow up poor? Poor compared to what? The only way you recognize your home is by recognizing all the other homes as not your home. Said another way: You are what you aren't. If you change the shape of a painting's background, you also change the shape of its subject.

Exercise: Seeing Stars

Can you see the star shape in each of the four quadrants below?

In watercolor painting, if you want lighter lights, you need to darken your darks. In life, we say we want lighter lights, but we run around trying to lighten our darks. Then the painting of life gets flatter and we wonder why. If we want to see our lights as lighter, we should preserve those darkest darks in the painting, where they can visibly stand apart and help define the lights. Good and evil aren't enemies. They're partners in a dance. We talk a big game about love, but don't seem to have the courage to love deeply enough to love the things we don't love. Sometimes you gotta dance with the one that brung ya.

A friend of mine told me a story about how his expectations of love were shot through so many times that he believed he had reached the bottom of the hole and could see that love didn't exist. Then he said he fell through the bottom of that hole, and could see how everything was an expression of love, down to his bedroom carpet. But now this summit of "everything is love" had become his new lofty expectation of love, which got shot through all over again and made him feel like a fool. I don't know if you feel enlightened or like a fool today, but I'm fairly certain that this dance is dancing on as we speak.

Story Time: The Firehose

It's summer of 2019. My Game A house of cards collapsed in January, and I've been falling down this rabbit hole for months. I'm now over my "grace period," which was characterized by constant 10/10 experiences (often several per day). It was like riding a non-stop wave of dopamine, and gave me a new appreciation for the expression "high on life." I was basically full-on tripping when stimulated by anything and everything. I'm not kidding when I say I was moved to tears by the sight of a man getting his $5 bill rejected by a vending machine.

I've now settled into a more chill version of Game B as a worldview, and am no longer experiencing daily—or even weekly—10/10s. I'm walking down the street one sunny afternoon and can feel one coming on. I don't get the sense that anything in particular has triggered it, but wow is it ever coming on. I stop to soak it in, can feel my skin tingling all over, and then get this very specific feeling that "god" is about to hit me with what I can only describe as a firehose of 10/10. BOOM. Absolutely ridiculous. My entire body is both numb and vibrating off the charts with this endorphin sensory overload.

Right when I felt like it couldn't possibly get any better, I get a strong feeling of "god" now leaning in and whispering: "Say when…" My mind suddenly opened to the idea that an all-powerful god would obviously have an infinite supply of 10/10 juice on tap. Not only was I given a taste, but I also 100% believed that I could ride that 10/10 for the rest of my life. It was mine for the taking if I wanted it. Who wouldn't want an endless supply of euphoric bliss?

What did I do? I stood there for roughly three minutes, ascending into nirvana. I then smiled and replied: "Okay, that's enough," then I dropped back down to a 2/10 experience. You heard that correctly. I actively chose the 2/10 over the 10/10, and the choice was obvious.

I tell this story to people and they think I'm insane. They all say they would opt for the infinite 10/10, but my gut says none of them would. It was a total no-brainer from a yin yang perspective. You can't have a 10/10 without a 2/10.

At the time, I was already on board with the concept of wanting 2/10s to contrast my 10/10s, but it was more of an abstract idea. It's one thing to engage in that thought experiment, and something else entirely to experience it in your bones.

Your greatest weakness is almost always also your greatest strength (and vice-versa). In *The Lord of the Rings*, the ring bearer must be someone like Frodo because he is so weak and unimportant. Were the ring to corrupt him, what would he become? Gollum? Bilbo? In the hands of Frodo, the worst case scenario isn't that bad for Middle Earth. Were the ring to corrupt a stronger character like Gandalf, Galadriel, or Aragorn, it would be capable of doing much more damage through them (their greatest strength is also their greatest weakness). Frodo is therefore important only by virtue of the fact that he is so unimportant. Picasso could paint like a traditional painter, but how many traditional painters who mocked him could paint like Picasso?

My brother recently painted a watercolor landscape featuring a lighthouse, which had extremely wonky proportions and looked like it belonged in a Tim Burton film. The flaws in the perspective and form of the structure are impossible to ignore, but they're also clearly the most interesting aspects of the piece. If he had straightened out the walls and given it more "correct" proportions, then the gains in realism would've come at the cost of its most distinctive qualities. It would've been another forgettable lighthouse landscape, and nowhere near memorable enough to reference in this book. Consider why Italy's Leaning Tower of Pisa is a tourist attraction. Now consider how your greatest weaknesses might also be your greatest strengths before you suck all of the soul out of your wonky lighthouses.

Take a walk in nature, and the value of wonky lighthouses becomes obvious. The tree that catches your eye is the one with all kinds of character. Bob Ross says "it's the imperfections that make something beautiful. That's what makes it different and unique from everything else." Watch one of his painting tutorials, and he warns against making all of your mountains perfect triangles and your trees perfectly straight. He invents stories for his trees. Maybe this one was stepped on when he was a sapling, and now he's got a crook in his back. Maybe this one is old and tired, so he leans against his friends for support.

That's not to say that a row of perfectly uniform trees isn't beautiful or interesting. My point is that nature doesn't make every tree to perfect exacting standards for a reason. It doesn't make people that way either. If someone stepped on your back when you were younger, that doesn't make you a broken person. That's your story, and what a story it is.

B3. What a ride/show

Life should not be a journey to the grave with the intention of arriving safely in a pretty and well preserved body, but rather to skid in broadside in a cloud of smoke, thoroughly used up, totally worn out, and loudly proclaiming 'Wow! What a Ride!'

— Hunter S. Thompson

If your life was a movie, would you want to watch it? If it was a game, would you want to play? Your knee-jerk response to these questions might be a hard "no," and yet...

Having just covered yin yang, we shouldn't be so quick to write off uninteresting or unpleasant movies and games. Depending on your state of mind, action movies can be boring, and boring movies can be action-packed. A bad movie clearly has value in my eyes, even if all of its worth is in its worthlessness. You're reading a book about literal nonsense as we speak. The performance art is strong.

Many of us spend our hard-earned money to see tragic plays and play horror video games. There has even been a recent rise in the popularity of simulator video games, in which the player goes about mundane tasks like cooking a meal or washing a car. Millions of people spend their free time watching YouTubers and Twitch streamers play these games, sometimes with no added commentary to make it more interesting. Why? I'm not sure, but I also spent a good chunk of my youth watching my brother play video games consisting mainly of fumbling around in menu screens. I found the games themselves terribly boring, but loved to watch. Here I sit, watching the memories of my younger self watching those games, thoroughly enjoying the show. I wonder if someone is currently enjoying the show of me writing about enjoying the show of watching myself watching those games. I suppose both of us are as we speak. Is anyone watching us? This is confusing... but also compelling. How do you write *that* script?

The ultimate method actor wouldn't even know that they were acting. It's funny how we get stage fright, when we're already performing on the biggest stage of all. As is illustrated in the above example, you don't need to live like a party animal or an overly dramatic actor in order to experience life as a ride or a show. While I find it much easier to see the performance art or ride-like qualities in more dramatic or exciting experiences, I also find it plain to see in more subtle experiences when I look for it. As is consistent with the other ideas in this book, I'm not talking about changing what is happening. I'm talking about a different perspective on what's already happening.

The idea that the gods envy us is not exactly new. The ancient Greeks arrived at this conclusion millennia ago, while most of us today run around trying to become gods. Aphrodite and Apollo must be sitting up there with popcorn in hand, captivated by the fact that the actors are trying to be the bored audience. The gods envy us envy the gods envy us envy the gods, and round and round we go!

After I began painting, I quickly began to see the world as a painting, noticing God's brushstrokes everywhere. I imagine many painters are jealous of the palette at God's disposal. The most expensive cerulean pigment pales in comparison to what you see when you look up at the sky on a clear day. God can paint with not only the most vibrant pigments, but also with scents, emotion, time, and the most subtle of gestures. When I was going through a period of appreciation for "God's brushstrokes," I would turn over a traffic cone just to marvel at a pebble underneath it. Why even bother putting that there? Because you can, of course. Another instance of the universe flexing. This incredible level of subtlety is all around you all the time. You couldn't notice it all if you wanted to. It's so ubiquitous that it's easy to sell people on the banality of day-to-day life. The painting is *too good*, which is why you don't see it. While Van Gogh was painting The Starry Night, the universe was effortlessly painting Van Gogh himself.

Why would the universe paint this particular ride that we're on? I'm not sure, but I think of it like doing a cosmic somersault because I can. You don't need to go to the edge of the universe to see something new. My brother experienced his spiritual awakening while he was living in Calgary, and was regularly blown away by what he referred to as "Calgary skies." He legitimately believed there was something about the city that made for incredible skies. Then he moved back to Ottawa, and saw that the skies were every bit as breathtaking here; he had just never looked up before.

We can romanticize all day about how pretty the sky is, but is that all there is? Are pretty skies the point of the ride? Yes? No? You don't care? I'm not the authority on what your ride is all about. I'm helplessly along for my own ride, and this is what that looks like. Even if some divine authority chimed in and told you that the ride is all about pretty skies, then you could totally ignore it and look down at the ground just to spite that dumb deity. If so, then you'd be helplessly along for the "don't tell me what my ride is all about" ride, which sounds like an intriguing ride to me. I wonder what *that* ride is all about. Where do I sign up? I can see why the gods might envy us.

Story Time: Toe Takes a Trip

An actual dog was trying to convince Toe to set his alarm for the middle of the night and get up for ten minutes just to mess with his sleep cycle. The dog said it had to do with "astrod protection," or something like that. Toe couldn't be bothered, so the actual dog set his alarm when he wasn't looking.

After a couple nights of annoying alarms, Toe found himself in a bout of sleep paralysis, with a demon sitting on his chest. Terribly unimpressed, Toe looked up and asked: "Uhhh, can I help you?" The demon, who fed exclusively on fear, replied: "Sorry. You mean you're not… This is awkward. I swear this never happens. I'll just go."

After the demon excused itself, Toe could hear deafeningly loud static, but just wanted to go back to bed. He then floated completely out of his own body, as he tried to claw his way back into his sheets. He drifted reluctantly out the window, where he thought there might be something odd, but he didn't bother to look. He flew through the night's sky and beyond the cosmos, landing in some kind of astral plane with arms folded.

Suddenly, Toe's higher self appeared. The actual dog said something about how your higher self is supposed to be, like, future-final-consciousness-stage-you, or the ultimate spirit guide, except for maybe angels or something.

"Hi. I'm you. Are you okay?" asked the actual god.

"Yeah I'm okay, I guess," replied Toe with a yawn.

"Okay, cool."

"Can I sleep now?"

Toe then woke up.

If you really were a god, you probably wouldn't just sit around and be infinite, eternal, and complete all day. For starters, you wouldn't even feel those things if you didn't *not* feel them sometimes. Otherwise, you'd be missing out on a whole subset of experiences, which hardly sounds complete to me. Infinity, eternity, and completeness could only be felt as the coming together of all now experiences, with each one filling in a piece of the whole. To "see everything as one" doesn't mean that all of the colors and shapes melt into one puddle of brown with no edges. It means seeing that the different colors are emphasized in relation to each other. The background and the foreground are one, in that each is necessary for the complete experience. The whole is the parts and the parts are the whole.

All of the different tones and instruments (silence included) make the music. All of the different materials make the instruments. All of the different physical processes make the materials. Don't forget that the players are also instruments themselves. The desire to play music drives them to get involved. The same desire drove the inventors to invent the instruments. Their heartbeats and physical capabilities drove those processes. I could go on and on, but we wouldn't do any of this if:

1. There was no one to listen to the music
2. We couldn't hear in the first place

Dancing is another excellent entry point into Game B insights. It allows us to get out of our heads and into our now experience in a visceral way not filtered through concepts. You might be locked up, struggle to find the "right" moves, or believe that "I can't dance." Forget all of that, and simply take your cues from the music. Let it dance you like a puppet. There are no "right" or "wrong" moves. There are just moves.

Dancing is actually the trigger that broke open my brother's dam when he was struggling to find what his dying patients were trying to tell him. He now has a reputation for dancing like an absolute jackass, but his style is so unlocked and free that everyone thinks it's legendary. People tell him "I wish I could dance like that," and he stresses that literally anyone can. You just have to let go and embrace the jackassery.

Exercise: Dancing Around It

Put on a favorite song of yours, put the damn book down, and dance in any way, shape, or form that feels right. Have some fun with it. You've earned it.

All of this happening so God can experience the 10/10 play from all of these points of view. Is this not a more infinite, eternal, and complete god than a god who just sits there and presides?

The tapestry is woven with such richness and complexity that it includes everyone passionately playing the "this isn't a game" game. They've got their part to play in this play, which happens to be playing the part of non-actors in a non-play. I've gotta say: The casting couldn't be better. A scene that is confoundingly complex for me to wrap my head around is effortless for the universe to perform. Maybe it's equally effortless for it to be confoundingly complex for me. God only knows.

Many Buddhists wish to become a buddha. Their goal is to meditate and control their thoughts and feelings until they feel nothing at all (effectively becoming a stone statue). They see the stone statues in temples as actual buddhas. I'd argue that the statues are images of buddhas meant to honor the real things. The real buddhas are people. They feel joy, judgment, and jealousy like you and I, because they *are* you and I. We recognize that a statue of Abraham Lincoln isn't the "real" man. I could argue that it is, but that's besides the current point. We don't think that the sign that says "Bank Street" is the "real" Bank Street. You wouldn't try to drive on the sign to reach your destination. Anyone who thinks a stone buddha is a statue of a stone buddha is confusing the finger for the Moon. I don't know about you, but becoming a stone statue sounds like a real bore. Who would want to go to an amusement park and feel nothing at all?

B4. Smelling the roses

And all your touch and all you see
Is all your life will ever be

— Pink Floyd (Breathe)

Picking up where we left off: If the stone buddha isn't a real buddha, then what is it? Surely, we can agree that it's a statue, since pretty much everyone would call it a statue. This would satisfy most adults, and they'd feel they've got around a 100% understanding of what it is, because it's a statue. Obviously. We're taught that the line of inquiry should end here, primarily for pragmatic reasons. To understand the problem with "why" questions, look up "Richard Feynman magnets" on YouTube. What happens if we keep digging, though? What do we actually mean when we say "statue"? If we call this thing in front of me "coffee cup," then what are we left with when we drop that label?

Exercise: Onoma-toe-poeia

Start tapping your toes on the ground like you're listening to a good song. Are you doing it yet? Just do it. We could say that "toe tapping" is a concept, while the *thud thud thud* you hear and feel right now is not a concept.

Activities like yoga, meditation, walking, or running seem to tune our conscious antenna off of the concept channel and onto the channel of raw experience. The familiar repetition allows us to slip into a trance that turns down our cognitive filters and amplifies our instincts. In that moment, you cease to be "running" and you become the *thud thud thud* of this other frequency coming in loud and clear. Osho says "this is not philosophy. This is the consequence of being silent." Most of us aren't capable of sitting in this silence. We can't help but explain away the noise with more noise. We can thank our love affair with sauce.

A child comes to you with genuine fear in their eyes and says "I saw a ghost." An adult might dismiss their fear by assuring them that "ghosts aren't real." But that fear is as real as the thing we call "coffee cup." When we say "fear," what we really mean is the event the child is currently experiencing. Having the experience of seeing a ghost *is* seeing a ghost. From this frame, how are ghosts not as real as this book or the color red?

Jonathan Pageau of *The Symbolic World* on YouTube has an excellent video in which he compellingly argues that Santa Claus and the tooth fairy "exist" in an obvious and very real way. You can go to a shopping center and actually interact with Santa Claus. You might say "that's not Santa; it's Joe in a Santa costume." Pageau explains that Joe is simply the tool through which Santa manifests himself in the world (in exactly the same way that your mouth is the tool through which you manifest your speech). Pageau says his young daughter understands that he places the money under her pillow because the tooth fairy makes him do it, so of course the tooth fairy is real.

If scientists detect a pattern of activity in your brain that they recognize as fear and you clarify that "at the time, I was actually feeling jealous," the scientists don't tell you that you're incorrect and were actually feeling fear. They go back and revise their model to account for the possibility of jealousy in that pattern of brain activity. When we say "fear," we don't mean this data on a chart of brain activity. What we *really* mean is something visceral and much less symbolic. Most people would say they're having an experience of reality, but I feel like their experience *is* reality.

Does anything exist outside of your now experience? If a tree falls in the woods and there's no one around to hear it, then does it make a sound? The answer is in this book, and the answer is that the answer isn't in this book. Lao Tzu did not write the Tao Te Ching about the Tao Te Ching, so clinging to the text will always lead you away from what the text is pointing at. Don't confuse the finger for the Moon.

Story Time: Toe Tells All

Toe is holding one of his week-long workshops, and you have been selected as one of the five lucky students. The topic of the workshop is "The Foundation of Game B."

The first lecture takes place on a patio in the evening. After everyone exchanges pleasantries, Toe gestures with his head to the full Moon in the sky and asks: "What is it?" As the first to respond, you tentatively offer the obvious answer: "The Moon…?" Knowing Toe's tendency to say "labels are a disaster," student two replies: "We couldn't call it 'the Moon,' since I see no letters up there." Student three recalls a Zen technique they heard about, pointing directly to it and answering: "That thing." Student four tries to mimic the silent Zen masters they've seen in movies, opting to say nothing at all. Student five, seeing an opportunity to borrow from his peers, points to it and says nothing. Toe then asks the group: "Are you satisfied?" Student five suddenly bursts into laughter.

You and three students eagerly await the next lesson at a cafe with pen and paper at the ready, but student five is missing. Toe doesn't wait for them and abruptly puts a full cup of coffee in the middle of the table. After obnoxiously spilling some of it onto your notes, Toe asks again: "What is it?" All four students simultaneously point to the cup without saying a word, answering: "   ." After a long pause, Toe asks the group: "Are you satisfied?" The students look around at each other, but no one is displaying confidence. You speak up: "Please tell us. What is it?" Toe points to the cup without saying anything, answering: "   ." After about a minute of this, student four exclaims "no way!" and proceeds to grab the cup, chug down the coffee, then exit the cafe with a serious case of the giggles. They obviously saw something, causing you to wonder: "Isn't it just a cup of coffee? What am I missing?"

You and the other two remaining students attend the rest of the workshop, which wraps up with a hike in the woods with no cameras or notebooks allowed. Hoping to apply what you learned, you spend the following weeks and months frantically pointing at the Moon and chugging coffee while remaining silent, except for the occasional bout of forced laughter.

Despite taking careful notes and doing everything you learned in the workshop, you can't seem to find the satisfying epiphany displayed by students four and five. Convinced you must have missed a crucial lesson on the hike, you compare notes with students two and three. Getting nowhere, the three of you sign up for every upcoming workshop with Toe, praying that you'll be lucky enough to be selected again.

My brother told me that one of his most meaningful experiences occurred while hiking in China's mountains. He said the hike itself was exaggerated, and the view awaiting them at the lookout was beyond exaggerated. As he feasted on the awe-inspiring visuals, other tourists asked him why he wasn't taking a photo. Surely, he was missing out... A year later, I was admiring the watercolor piece he painted from his memory of the view, which was hanging on the wall in his home. I wonder how many photos taken by those tourists remain buried in their camera rolls, never to be looked at again. Most of them never even looked at the view in the first place.

It'd be nice if we could view the views without being aware of "viewing the views," which seems to block the view altogether. I feel like this is the way children see the world, before they're converted into ringwraiths. We're handed a rose, then feel like we need to do some chore in order to make the most out of smelling it. But doing the chore to make the most out of smelling it isn't smelling it, which is what we ultimately want. Why do we make everything so hard on ourselves? Just smell the rose. Now would be a good time to take a sip of your beverage. Forget about "sipping" and just sip.

Story Time: The Unsipped Beers Part II

> Taylor and Alex are actually puppets controlled by Morgan, a performance artist who loves the image of the unsipped beers. Experiencing the unsipped beers through Taylor and Alex is like sipping on a cold beer to Morgan.

So is smelling the roses therefore where it's at? Not exactly. Too much focus on smelling the roses and you'll miss the smell of the weeds. A Hollywood celebrity might be so focused on "making it" that they don't stop to sip the flavors they encounter along their journey to the top. Once they've made it, they might look back on the "good old days" of waiting tables with nostalgia, missing the feeling of a sore back or the taste of cheap diner coffee. They realize that once you've made it to the peak of success, the air still tastes the same up there. Few of us are rich with the kind of money, status, or power that movie stars have, but everyone is rich with poor man's gold.

> He said a fool's ambition is all you know
> There ain't no dollar gonna make you whole
> There ain't no telling what you've been told
> But your money won't buy you no poor man's gold
>
> "Poor Man's Gold" (Jamestown Revival)

Ever notice how wealthy people can be horribly depressed and poor people can be beaming with joy? It's funny how we don't recognize them as the "good old days" when we're in them. The rich rockstar was likely sold a story that sipping on champagne would save them. When it doesn't, their cognitive dissonance kicks in. When you believe that value = dollars, then you tend not to value the beauty in nature and life because it was given to us for free. While they aren't wrong that the *champagne* sipping lifestyle is expensive, their blind spot is missing that the sipping lifestyle is free. Anyone can sip a sunset, a breeze, or the song of a bird. But what if that sensation is painful? Who wants to sip on heartbreak or a sore back? Let's not forget about yin yang.

If you're paying attention, then the pebble in your shoe can be just as beautiful and moving as a sunset, but to most it's "just a pebble." After I began painting, I gained a new appreciation for still life pieces. It's all too easy to think we've got something ordinary like a banana figured out. We look at a still life painting of a banana, think "nice banana painting," and move on. But when was the last time you *really* looked at one of those things? That artist had to engage on a level far deeper than "banana" to convey what they saw (probably noticing colors, textures, and shapes that would surprise you). You don't need to go to Mars to see something new. Pick up a banana and experience it.

A terminal illness diagnosis or a near-death experience is often the kick that people need to smell the roses in a non-ringwraith way. You've probably heard anecdotes of people quitting their jobs or having radical worldview shifts after a brush with death. While these stories may be moving or inspiring, I worry that most of us are only capable of interpreting them from our ringwraith perspective, and any changes they inspire are merely a doubling down on Game A.

Someone might be swapping a career improvement game for a spiritual or family improvement game, thinking they're making a huge change. I see this as a sort of hollow realization, where the perceived massive change amounts to little more than trading in your parachute for a shiny new hang glider… but more on that later. Maybe I can expedite a deeper realization for you without having to drop you out of a plane…

Exercise: Final Thoughts

Suppose there's a bomb whistling overhead (imagine the sound). You can hear it and you know that in one minute, you're finished. Everyone who matters already knows that you love them and your goodbyes have all been said.

NOW: Set a timer and play it out.

If your life was grossly limited, would it still have meaning? This can be a very difficult question for the player of Game A, whose meaning is tied up in actualizing the potential of tomorrow, rather than smelling the roses of today. If you lived forever, you'd never again be able to smell a rose for the first time. You'd never again feel the full force of having your heart broken as a teenager and thinking your life is over. You'd never again get to experience the birth of your first child. You'd never again get to learn how to fly as a bird or a bat or a bee. You want the meaning without the limitation, but the limitation *is* the meaning. We all see the value in those big first events of life, romanticizing them with ceremonies and celebrations. Why don't we see the same value in our last kiss, our last meal, or our last sunset? The rose is worth smelling *because* it dies, and because *we* die.

How is it that we view death as an ugly problem, but have no issue seeing the beauty all around us every autumn. As far as I can tell, everything in nature conforms to cycles of birth and death. Why should we be any different? From this perspective, it's clearly both natural and necessary. It's almost like nature knows what it's doing, and we're overcomplicating our lives by trying to outsmart it. We want to smell the roses of the colorful autumn leaves, but we don't want to change colors ourselves. Why wouldn't the process be just as vibrant and moving for us to experience? Maybe the leaves want to die just as much as we want them to. Listen to "Last Leaf" by Tom Waits, and you'll see the tragic side of unnaturally prolonged life. It's funny how we want to outsmart nature, but we *are* nature.

B5. The weather

This is how it is now... and this is how it is now.

— Anonymous

My two year old nephew was talking on the phone with his great uncle, who mentioned something about Lego bricks. My nephew responded by peering into his toy chest and exclaiming: "Maybe Lego coming!" The image of him wondering whether a new toy might magically appear in his room based on something he was told on the phone might look silly to you. And yet, we regularly wonder whether a new storm might magically appear in the sky based on something we were told on the radio. Maybe storms coming!

We have a tendency to focus on "the way things are" as if it's a fixed state and see problems as things that need to be actioned out of in order to arrive at a solution. When the only tool you own is a hammer (the habit of 'I can do things'), then every problem looks like a nail. Consider any problem that comes to mind (political, professional, personal, etc.), and now consider doing absolutely nothing about it (without considering whether or not doing nothing is doing something). Will the problem eventually resolve itself? You may not like what that resolution looks like, but that problem will resolve itself too. You don't need to force winter to turn into spring. Try your hardest to stop spring from coming and watch what happens.

I was recently in a debate with a friend, and they argued that "you're still gonna go to work on Monday." This position sounds like a Game A foil to my "try and stop spring from coming" point, and this is my carefully considered response: I concede that if you show up to my office on Monday, you'll almost certainly find me there working. However, I in no way need to "go to work" in order to be there. If you've ever been daydreaming or distracted while walking and then arrived at your destination with no recollection of the journey, then you'll understand what I'm getting at. You might have experienced this phenomenon while driving. Someone else would likely look at you and say "they're walking somewhere," while your experience of the event might be "watching the sunset from Mars." Both explanations would be 100% consistent despite being 33.9 million miles apart.

Exercise: The Weatherman

Your friend firmly believes that they can control the weather. They've become upset with their recent weather controlling performance, and have come to you for advice.

a) What will you tell them? Write down you main point(s)

b) Look at the language in your response. How do you sound?

Your friend says "I hear what you're saying and I wish to become more like you. How do I make *my* control of the weather more like *yours*?"

c) What will you tell them now? How do you sound?

I'm not advocating for letting go of the wheel in all aspects of your life, or suggesting that *this* is the way things are. I'm trying to show how if you change your perspective on any given subject, your experience of that subject will likely start to adapt to your new perspective. If you see life as a series of tasks that need to be performed, then you'll see a whole lot of doing that needs to get done. If you see life as a completely passive event unfolding, then you'll start seeing many of your "actions" as automatic and effortless. Neither perspective is "right" or "wrong," in the same way that the color blue is neither right nor wrong.

There's a modern obsession with willing things. Consider the Taoist principle of "wu wei," which translates to "non-action." It's typically understood as an instruction: "Let things take their own course." I'm convinced that this is a mis-translation (not Chinese-to-English, but due to a different culture 2,000 years ago when it was said). I believe that Lao Tzu meant it as a statement: "Action doesn't exist." You don't need to let things take their own course because they already are. Again: Please demonstrate your ability to interfere with this process. It doesn't surprise me that the message meant to relieve people from their obsession with willing things is understood by people as yet another thing that needs to be willed.

From the perspective of "action doesn't exist," the weather-like happenings of the world—as one experiences them—are completely consistent. This makes perfect sense to me. However, nearly every time I present the idea of a life lived completely on autopilot, I'm met with a response that "if people really lived that way, then nothing would get done!" They completely miss the point that it's *already* happening that way. I'm not talking about a change in the way people act. I'm talking about a perspective change on what's already going on.

Story Time: Far Gone Fred

My friend Fred is desperate to have his cup filled, but he still doesn't understand how to fill it on his own.

We're having a heavy vaping session tonight, and Fred is particularly stoned. We decide to go for a walk, but I'm a little concerned about Fred's far gone state.

On our walk, we get the idea that it would be fun to enter this lively looking pub nearby. The plan is to go in, sit at the bar, and get one drink. This plan may not sound very daunting, but it's ambitious given the circumstances.

Upon entering, we sit at the busy bar, and manage to get waters and menus. We each select a fancy cocktail, which is a lot to ask of Fred right now. So far so good.

The server taking our order asks for our ID, and I'm carrying nothing but cash on me. Fred is now visibly freaking out. I thank our server, tip my imaginary hat to the others now staring at us, grab Fred, and get out of there.

Walking home, Fred says he feels horrible about the ordeal. I remind him that we technically accomplished our plan to perfection. We went in, sat at the bar, and got one drink. The drink happened to be water, and we got more drama than we bargained for, but we also got to share an experience that was memorable enough to share with you. Our cups runneth over.

You can get so wrapped up in your expectation of "ordering a drink at the bar" that you miss the actual experience, since it doesn't look like what you were expecting. The rainy day only sucks because you had hopes for a sunny day. When today's planned picnic is canceled, your image of today dies. You might say "today isn't going according to plan," but I would beg to differ. We become so focused on an imagined today that we slam the door on the today we have (the only one we ever have). Most of us can't fill our own cups because we wouldn't recognize a full cup if we saw one. Our cups are so full with perceived emptiness that there isn't any room left in them for fullness. Everyone wants their cup filled, but few realize that they can fill it themselves for free. You can fill up on poor man's gold whenever you want, but H.G. Tannhaus in *Dark* (2017) warns of one small caveat: "You can choose as you want, but your wants are chosen for you."

Much like the weather, the switch controlling this perspective shift doesn't appear to be controllable. It flips itself when it's ready, which can be frustrating if you want to change your perspective today. Perhaps we can change our perspective on our ability to change our perspective. We seem to understand that we can't control whether or not today is a sunny day. We may complain when we wake up to a rainy day, but we accept that there's no use in fighting it. We grab an umbrella and go about our day. The sun will come out if and when it's ready. The way to wake up to a sunny day is to wait for it to happen. The same method applies with this perspective shift. You may be going about one of your days waiting for it to flip, only to realize that it has somehow already happened. The switch flipped itself when you weren't looking.

The more I started looking at my problems the way I look at the weather, the more my problems started to look like the weather. I noticed that many of my problems would 100% solve themselves with zero effort on my part. I imagine many would call this "manifestation." Said another way: "This too shall pass." For example, I felt like I needed to eliminate my anxiety symptoms in order to enjoy my day. However, this approach was like trying to fight the rainy day. It *is* raining and I *am* anxious, and that's okay. Much like grabbing an umbrella, I can take a deep breath and enjoy my day as an anxious person. Not surprisingly, my symptoms became much more manageable when I accepted them as a passing storm. My brother once told me that "people who go to the doctor are infinitely more likely to have an illness." It took me a long time to see what he meant.

I remember my brother telling me that the shift in my language was a clear sign that my experiences were filtering through this other worldview. Instead of talking about "digging deep" or "really focusing" on the connectedness I was feeling from art and yoga at the time, I described "tuning my antenna" and "getting out of my own way." There's a distinct flavor of passivity, surrender, and reception, rather than self-actualization, control, and expression. "Tuning your antenna" is particularly fitting, because although you can tune your antenna, you can't control the signal it receives. It's the same kind of passivity with which one grows their hair. You can stop cutting it (like the active component of tuning your antenna), but beyond that, all you can do is wait and see what nature brings.

I feel like many of us could use a break from all that willing and doing in order to connect back in with our surroundings. While hiking with my brother one summer, I noticed him pausing to do what looked like a type of meditation. Afterwards, I realized he was taking the time to get out of his own way and boost his antenna's reception. The following winter, I attended a yoga class on a cold morning, and engaged in a similar exercise in passivity while sitting and waiting for class to begin. I was staring out the window at the hustle and bustle on the street, and felt every bit as connected to the man scraping the ice off of his car as I did to the floor beneath me. I was him, and he was me. That moment has passed, and so will we. Life makes a lot more sense to me when I see myself as the passing clouds. According to Ram Dass, "everything changes once we identify with being the witness to the story, instead of the actor in it."

B6. The red pill

I think everybody should get rich and famous and do everything they ever dreamed of so they can see that it's not the answer.

— Jim Carrey

We think we know what we want, but I think we haven't thought it through. One of the most mind blowing Game B insights I had was this idea that you're always getting exactly what you want... You just have no idea what you want. I call this "cosmic want," as opposed to conscious want. This notion is extremely hard to wrap your mind around from a Game A point of view, but it's as simple as it sounds.

Oddly enough, I arrived at this conclusion during a very unpleasant day of throwing up with a stomach bug. Why would anyone want that? It was most definitely a miserable experience, and yet I could plainly see a *much* deeper layer of how I might crave the misery of it all. This insight didn't make it any less miserable, but it allowed me to savor the misery in all of its miserableness. It was as if I both wanted out and in at the same time, but these interests didn't have to compete. I could see both sides, and neither had to win over the other. They just were.

My feeling is that the world is made by someone or something much smarter than us. If we could be god in a Game A sense, we'd make a world that makes us god in a Game B sense (exactly like the one we're experiencing now). I suspect the most advanced forms of life want to be us, which is why things are the way they are. From my point of view, we're already living the leveled up version of the dream, as we run around wishing to level up. What a deep and nuanced version of living the dream. If we had everything we wished for, we'd be robbed of the fun of the wishing.

If all you did was win, wouldn't that be the dream? Careful what you wish for. It might turn out to be a nightmare. In *The Nightmare Before Christmas* (1993), Jack Skellington experiences what I describe as "God's problems." While everyone wants to be him, all he wants is to be is anyone else:

> But who here would ever understand
> That the Pumpkin King with the skeleton grin
> Would tire of his crown, if they only understood
> He'd give it all up if he only could

> "Jack's Lament" (Danny Elfman)

If you've ever played a video game on "god mode," you've probably noticed how it's fun to be invincible for a while, but it gets boring fast. You'd get no thrill out of beating Super Mario if every dangerous pit was boarded up and the bad guys didn't bite. It's understandable that we complain about the obstacles and setbacks we face in life, but we don't stop to consider the alternative. Maybe God doesn't have any problems, which is precisely God's problem. Don't be so quick to wish away your worries. It'd be a woeful world without worries.

Imagine if you could remember what it was like to be every living and non-living thing in the universe. You would have a perfect memory of what it was like to be every person, every creature, every grain of sand, etc. That would be amazing... until it wasn't. If you could remember *everything*, you'd likely crave the ability to forget it all. At that point, the thing you'd wish for more than anything else would be a button labeled "SURPRISE," which would lead you to exactly where you are now, wondering what it would be like to remember those things you begged to forget. The surprise game has one distinctive feature that may give it an edge over all other games: It resets. Right when you think you've seen it all and this game has run its course... Surprise!

Cultural conditioning causes us to forget our belief in magic, because "magic isn't real." Notice how babies seem to marvel in wonder at the simplest things. For them, the wrapping paper is just as enthralling as the gift inside. For me, seeing Game B caused less of a realization of something new, and more of a remembering of my prior belief in magic. This idea that everything is magic is now intuitive to me, to the point that it's obvious. However, when I was in the process of sliding down this rabbit hole, "ordinary" things started transforming before my eyes into pure magic. I imagine this is what tripping on psychedelic drugs is like, allowing you to access this more raw way of seeing the world by removing the thick lenses of your conceptual conditioning.

Exercise: The Magician

You encounter a street magician with a distinctive face, who offers to perform their "magic mirror" trick for you. You oblige, and the magician sits you down inside a booth in front of a frame covered by a curtain. The curtain is drawn and you're face-to-face with a perfect reflection in the image of the magician. Your every move and blink is matched with uncanny perfection by the distinctive face before you. The curtain closes. What just happened?

a) You just experienced actual magic; the magician is a true master of technique and performance.

b) You just experienced actual magic; you were looking in a normal mirror, but hallucinated the magician's face.

c) You just experienced actual magic; both you and the magician happened to mirror each other by impossible coincidence.

d) You just experienced actual magic; you just experienced all of the above thanks to your powerful imagination.

NOW: Draw the magician's face.

Many of us are so tuned to the language of words and concepts that our antennas don't even pick up the language of nature. A friend of mine says when she doesn't know what to do, she asks a tree, and finds great wisdom in the rustling of the leaves. It's almost as if the answer saying nothing about your problem is saying that your problem is nothing. Now consider how most people with culturally conditioned thinking wouldn't hear any answer at all to their question were they to receive a response of rustling leaves.

From my perspective, nature's answer is screaming loud and clear, and is infinitely better than any words I can string together in this book. And yet it's "just the leaves," and might as well be deafening silence to those seeking a collection of words in response. This reminds me of a story I heard about former Canadian prime minister Pierre Trudeau. He went for a walk on a cold winter night while wrestling with the decision of whether to retire from politics. According to a CBC News report, he said "I went out to see if there were any signs of my destiny in the sky, but there weren't… There was nothing but snowflakes." The universe is singing for you. Are you listening? When I put someone on the spot with this question, I'm sometimes met with an authentic and vulnerable "no." I then get the sense that they're going to spend a lot of time thinking about it.

"Bone belief" is one of the deeper concepts I arrived at after an absurd amount of my own pondering. Much like cosmic want, this level of belief operates much deeper than our surface-level thoughts. Throughout your life, you've been sold a bunch of ideas, some of which you now believe at an extremely deep level. Bone belief has to do with those beliefs held so deeply that you don't even question them. For example, you probably believe that you can get up in the morning. You don't question whether or not you got up this morning. It's self-evident.

True belief occurs when it's not even on the table. I'm talking about the difference between 99.99999999% belief and 100% belief, which is the difference between incomplete and complete belief. Any sliver of doubt puts it back on the table. If you were to start questioning whether or not you got up this morning, then it couldn't be considered a bone belief (unless you bone believed it could). As far as I can tell, you can't consciously convince yourself into a bone belief. I'm guessing this is because to engage with the notion of whether you believe something at all is to keep it on the table. If you actually believed it at 100%, you wouldn't need to convince yourself of anything.

In *The Matrix*, no one is able to convince Neo that he is the One, yet there comes a moment when it's obvious to him that he is. He doesn't have to convince himself that he can stop bullets, like how he tried and failed to convince himself that he could fly in the jump training simulation. Once it comes off the table and he bone believes that he is the One, he simply looks at the bullets and says "no." Please don't go jumping off of buildings and in front of bullets because Toe said something about the power of belief. I just think Neo offers an excellent (albeit exaggerated) example of what bone belief looks like.

You're probably not convinced, and might wonder what happens when someone encounters something that contradicts their held bone belief. Does that mean their initial bone belief was mistaken? The simplest explanation I can think of is that the belief has moved from off the table to on the table, so it's no longer a held bone belief. If they bone believe that their initial bone belief was mistaken, then it was mistaken, since the belief about the belief is now off the table. It's actually quite simple, as long as you consider whether the belief is on or off the table.

This concept becomes difficult to understand when we run into conflicting perspectives. If I bone believed I was hovering a foot in the air, and I passed someone who bone believed I was walking on the ground, then who would be correct? For a moment, forget about any notion of objective reality. Don't get hung up on labels of "correct" or "true," and consider each of the perspectives presented. I bone believe that I'm floating, so I am. I don't even question it. They bone believe that I'm not floating, so I'm not. They don't even question it. Both realities are completely consistent without any issues whatsoever. Perspectives don't need to agree in conversations, so why should they need to agree when it comes to realities? If your knee-jerk reaction is that "believing something doesn't make it true," then my knee-jerk response would be "it sounds like you believe that…"

All the red pill does is get you off of the immediate "Game A" ride. Mind blowing as that may be, it doesn't save you, and it leaves many stuck with an even bigger problem than the impossibility of winning at the improvement game: Now what? Once you start seeing Game B insights, it's hard to unsee them, or climb back up the slide. While I don't doubt that you could be conditioned back into a culturally consistent worldview, Game B perspectives seem to not require any conditioning, and flow more easily once there's a crack in the dam.

I've noticed an annoying phenomenon: If you introduce a new point of view to someone, they often ask you to prove it. First of all, their current point of view was never proven. It was inherited from their parents and culture. Second of all, how could a point of view ever be proven? A point of view is like a recipe. Cooking competitions don't judge a recipe on the cook's explanation of why it's the best. The judges simply taste it for themselves. The proof is in the pudding of their experienced taste of the recipe, not their conceptual understanding of it.

What I find striking is the reluctance of most adults to sample new recipes when it comes to worldviews. They cling to their conditioned perspective because their very existence is staked on it. Given the option of eating an eternity of comforting gruel or feasting like a king and then dying, most people reach for the gruel (while resenting those feasting). Alan Watts says "it's better to have a short life that is full of what you like doing than a long life spent in a miserable way."

If you love the gruel, then that's great. Enjoy it. Just know that you don't *have* to eat it. You're free to sample from the rich and varied buffet of life at any time. I'd go as far as to say you're already sampling from it, but you don't stop to savor the tastes. We only notice the taste when we're eating the gruel, and then we wonder why our lives are so mundane. Variety is the spice of life. If all you ever knew was chocolate ice cream, then "plain" old vanilla wouldn't be plain at all. It would blow your mind.

Story Time: The Consistent Curator

Courtney is the curator of an art gallery dedicated to impressionism. She loves impressionism and despises cubism. She has never liked a cubist painting and is sure she never will.

She recently began actively avoiding cubist pieces in order to save herself the wasted time.

One night, Courtney became stuck in a strange dream. She was locked in a room with two pieces on display: A Monet and a Picasso. The only thing she could do was look at either of the paintings to pass the time, which seemed to stretch on forever.

How long until Courtney gives the Picasso a chance? How long until she loves it?

A life lived entirely confined to the flavor of Game A seems sad to me. Most of us love watching children try a new food for the first time. I love watching people get that first taste of what I'm talking about. I never get tired of hearing the stories. That said, if the world was completely immersed in Game B, I'd likely make it my mission to give people a taste of Game A.

We all recognize the pitfalls of monotony, and yet we have a tendency to keep reaching for the gruel, day after day. We pretend not to see the buffet of delicacies within our reach. We avoid other points of view like the plague, because deep down, we know that our own recipe is no good. The flavor is awful. The texture is awful. The aftertaste is awful. The experience of the meal is awful, but the *idea* of it is wonderful. It's familiar. It's comforting. It reinforces our beliefs. So we keep our heads down and pretend it's delicious. No pain, no gain. It's a perfectly valid approach to living that serves us just fine… until it doesn't.

When the gruel finally fails to deliver on its promises of improvement or salvation, then all we are left with is the awful taste. Neo chooses the red pill because he knows there's something wrong with his current meal plan. The good news is that you have other options. As luck would have it, I've saved you a seat at the buffet. Care to join?

Story Time: Members Only

Your friend tells you about a new club in town called YOUniverse that everyone is talking about. They make you go through a rigorous application process in order to receive the photo ID membership card required to grant you access. Your curiosity gets the better of you, and you begin filling out the long application form. The questions are extremely esoteric and you're not sure how there could be any cohesive criteria upon which you could be evaluated. Rather than trying to figure it out, you quickly complete the form and submit it, hoping that maybe you got lucky and did it exactly right.

The next week, you receive an envelope in the mail from YOUniverse. You don't recall ever giving your address, so you assume it's just promotional material. Inside, however, is your personal photo ID membership card complete with your eye color, hair color, and favorite color. Your photo on the card is both new to you and extremely flattering. When and how did they take it? Your friend reports that they also received their card, and the two of you plan to attend on Friday evening.

All week, you can't help but keep admiring your card. You keep pulling it out every chance you get, until you notice that the top layer containing your photo and personal information is starting to peel. Before you know it, you've compulsively ripped off the sticker, which is no longer sticky at all. Now you've done it. All that's left of your custom card is the generic template.

Friday night arrives, and you're waiting in line with your friend. You notice the bouncer is carefully vetting each card against its holder. You can't think of a clever strategy, and decide to simply hope the bouncer is too distracted to notice the lack of photo or any identifying info on your card. Your friend offers theirs, which the bouncer carefully studies. He then opens the rope and your friend enters. You hand the bouncer your card, and to your dismay, he studies it as carefully as all the others. He then opens the rope and waves you in.

Game B summary

Now that you have a sense of what Game B is about, you might see how when it's viewed from a Game A perspective, Game B looks a lot like Game A being played poorly. Someone who thinks baseball is the only sport in town would look at someone playing basketball and say "no offense, but you're really terrible at baseball. Let me help you. I'll show you how to play correctly." Game A tends to dismiss Game B ideas as "lazy," "ridiculous," and "irresponsible" because it's trying to apply a frame to a painting that doesn't match. It's judging basketball players by the rules of baseball. It's saying that all paintings should fit this frame, because this is the only frame in town. Game B says there are other frames and there are other games.

Game A is like painting yourself to match your frame, whereas Game B is like painting your frame to match yourself. When you see the world as you are, then it starts looking pretty magical. This magic is difficult to see through all those frames we've had imposed on us to explain what we're looking at. Once you stop looking through those, then it becomes a natural response to marvel at whatever you're looking at.

I could describe 10/10 experiences as religious in nature for the person experiencing them, but what does this Game B phenomenon look like from a Game A perspective? I often think about the story of Moses and the burning bush, and how another eyewitness might describe the event. We have a tendency to embellish stories of our experiences, and these stories tend to become even more exaggerated as we pass them down as myths and legends. Today, we tell the burning bush story as if it was an awe-inspiring sight to behold, complete with supernatural effects and voiceover worthy of a divine provenance.

While I don't doubt the burning bush experience was magical and enrapturing from Moses's perspective, my hunch is that our eyewitness would describe the entire event as entirely uneventful: "It was just a dude looking at a totally normal bush. I don't get it," they might testify. Those of us lucky enough to have had an earth-shattering 10/10 experience while looking at something "ordinary" will know exactly what I mean. The thing itself doesn't change. How you see it changes.

Game B insights simply don't translate into any kind of sense from a Game A point of view. In the 2019 documentary *American Factory*, there's a scene in which the camera happens to catch what I'm convinced is an enlightening mystical experience for an American factory worker. While in China, he realizes that although eastern and western cultures may differ, there's plenty of overlap, and we're ultimately the same. Not surprisingly, he struggles immensely to put it into words, is overcome with emotion, and immediately tries to share his insight with the next people he encounters. They laugh off his comment and politely dismiss him. His sincere attempt to explain their connectedness appears to drive them further apart.

Closer to home, one of my yoga teachers (michaeldynie.com) said the following about his practice as he ages: "I'm enjoying watching this slowly slip away from me." That's one of the most Game B things I've ever heard. I see all six pillars in that one short sentence. By focusing so much on getting the goodie, we can't see that losing it *is* having it.

The Jungle

Illustration by Red Raven Dances

What is the Jungle?

The Jungle is a common spiritual, existential, or philosophical crisis that occurs when we don't want to play Game A anymore, but we don't know how to stop.

I've listed below what I feel are the six pillars of the Jungle, which will be explored in this section. Consider this your warning that the concepts ahead are philosophically dense and challenging. That said, I think there's immense value in attaching a name to this common spiritual crisis. Knowing some of the tricks in the mind's playbook could help to shorten your stay in this maddening mental maze.

Jungle pillars:

1. Fake Game B
2. House of cards
3. Running out of road
4. Grasping at smoke
5. But how? (still the habit)
6. The tough pill to swallow

The tension between the desired outcome of dropping Game A and inability to move toward it produces the primary feature of the Jungle: Wobble. You can usually tell when someone is in the Jungle, because they become trapped in a mental tug-of-war that spills into their appearance, mood, and conduct. It looks like a form of defeated frustration, like a wolf caught in a leg trap. When coupled with the looping nature of our monkey minds, this wobble keeps feeding itself into a holding pattern of anxiety.

It's okay to be anxious. Just don't be anxious about being anxious. I'm not a doctor, but can speak from my experience as an anxious person. My understanding is that the worst treatment for anxiety is anything that avoids it. While avoiding it might work for a period, it gives the anxiety more power over you by reacting to it, and does nothing to address your inability to sit with it the next time it comes up. Like with any phobia, exposure therapy allows us to sit with the thing we're avoiding. In *Breaking Bad* (2008), Walter White testifies that "ever since my [cancer] diagnosis, I sleep just fine." There's something to be said for having the worst case scenario play out, so you can see that it's not the end of the world. Even if it is, then this too shall pass.

Personally, I noticed that my anxiety only ever presents as symptoms that make me anxious. As soon as I get used to a symptom enough that it no longer makes me anxious, then my anxiety will stop presenting as that symptom. Next thing I know, some new symptom pops up somewhere else. If this doesn't bother me, then my anxiety will poke and prod elsewhere in search of something that does worry me. If it manages to find something, then it latches on until I stop caring about that. As long as you're anxious about your anxiety, then your anxiety about your anxiety will continue to make you anxious.

These kinds of positive feedback loops are everywhere in the Jungle. The more you try to drop Game A, the more you end up recommitting to Game A. The more you try to understand how little you understand, the more understanding gets in the way of your non-understanding. When you grasp at smoke, the grasping itself kills the smoke. Then you think the answer is not to grasp, but now you're grasping for not grasping. Then you think the answer is to kill your ego, but as a good friend of mine pointed out: Trying to kill your ego seems like a pretty ego-driven pursuit.

Exercise: Von Kleist's Boxing Bear

> A man is in a boxing match with a bear. The bear reads the man's mind and counters every move that he makes perfectly. They've been fighting for ages and the man has never made any hint of progress toward hitting the bear.
>
> How can the man hit the bear?

For simplicity's sake (as if that's possible in this section), think of the Jungle as an extremely highbrow version of Game A. I suppose one difference is that most people in the Jungle have had a more potent taste of Game B, which tends to be the driving force behind their desire to drop Game A. That said, plenty of people locked in Game A slip into

Game B states every now and then. They just don't recognize Game B as an alternative game available to them. There's so much overlap between Game A and the Jungle that I want to call them identical, but the Jungle is also distinct enough in my view to deserve an entire section dedicated to exploring its intricate facets and features. When you're in the Jungle, it may feel completely different than the Game A that you're used to. However, underneath its convoluted complexity, it's effectively the same game by another name.

J1. Fake Game B

I really don't know life at all

— Joni Mitchell (Both Sides Now)

Whichever lens you observe the world through will color what you see, since looking through a lens is also looking directly at it. This phenomenon seems especially true of Game A, which fiercely repackages everything it encounters into improvement terms. Playing Game B for Game A reasons is still just Game A by another name. It's a game I like to call "fake Game B."

Someone looking to drop Game A might say "I'm not broken and I don't need to be fixed." Sounds like Game B to me. Then they follow with a statement like "the *system* is broken and needs to be fixed," and that "unity must win over division." Sound familiar?

After spending some time in Denmark, a friend of mine was raving about the concept of Hygge. She said it's a lifestyle built on minimalism and the idea of enjoying the simple things in life, like a cup of coffee or a glass of wine. It sounds a lot like poor man's gold to me, and a classic Game B motivation. However, she was saying that this lifestyle makes Denmark the "ideal place to be," since "you look at the people here, and they're all genuinely happy." Suddenly, this other lifestyle is starting to look like a means of chasing happiness, perfection, and improvement.

I'm in no way knocking my friend or this lifestyle (they're both wonderful). I'm trying to show how Game A takes obvious Game B motives and twists them to fit its motives. Game A-driven Hygge might leave someone feeling lost on the days when the simple pleasures aren't pleasurable, or feeling guilty after a less-than-minimalist shopping spree, which would otherwise be a genuine source of pleasure.

I do some things for Game B reasons that most people do for Game A reasons. For example, someone might take better care of their teeth not because they want to improve, but because they enjoy having cleaner teeth. Someone else might be less motivated to practice good oral hygiene under the weight of Game A's pressure to improve, subconsciously thinking their teeth should not be good enough like the rest of them. Someone playing Game B might appear more driven and disciplined than you might expect, and someone playing Game A might appear more lazy and lax. Leave some space for nuanced interpretation with these things.

I currently go to yoga eight times per week because I enjoy it. People say that I must be driven, dedicated, and disciplined to maintain such a demanding practice. I tell them it's 100% effortless from my perspective. I don't have this huge weight of having to perform on my shoulders all the time, and I'm not worried that I'm going to feel like I'm regressing if I skip a day. I'm not working toward anything, because I'm obviously already there. That was totally a lie… I'm working on my handstand right now, but I'm pursuing it because it's fun. I go to class for the same reason that a child goes to the playground. Do it every day for fun for three years, and you'll get really good at it while you enjoy the process. Force yourself to do it once a week for three years because you think it will save you, and you won't get nearly as good at it while you suffer through the process.

Story Time: Parachutes

You're kicked out of a plane at 20,000 feet up without a parachute. While you have a vague sense that you'll hit the ground some time in the future, you can't see it through the clouds and you're having too much fun twisting in the wind to even care at this point.

After the first thousand feet of falling, you break through the clouds and can now see the ground below. It's very far away, but you start thinking about the eventual need for a parachute as you continue to enjoy the feeling of the wind in your face.

At 18,000 feet, you get more serious about your predicament, and decide that you can make your own parachute if you just work hard enough. You spend the next couple thousand feet focused on the task, and you feel a sense of pride upon completing it. It's not much, but it's yours and it will save you.

At 16,000 feet, you deploy your parachute successfully and breathe a sigh of relief. You spend some time looking up and admiring your work, anticipating the breathtaking views during your safe and slow descent.

Expecting that you're now somewhere around 15,000 feet, you look down, and to your horror, see that you're at 8,000 feet and in free fall. How is this possible??

You look back up and see no parachute above you. There never was one. You imagined the whole thing. You spend the next thousand feet kicking yourself for being such an idiot, when a man swoops in on a hang glider. He's wearing a parachute of his own, and graciously offers to sell you his glider.

His price is steep, but no cost is too high for your salvation, as the ground is now close and rapidly approaching. You sell your soul to the man and grab a tight grip on the glider. This time, you *really* feel a sense of relief wash over you, as you close your eyes and thank the stars.

Excited to finally see those views, you open your eyes, and are shocked to see that you're now at 1,000 feet from impact and are once again in free fall. There never was a hang glider. Of course there wasn't. The ground is so close now that you don't have time to kick yourself or worry about it.

Even if you had a real parachute, it would be too late to deploy it. Despite your wasted efforts and mistakes, you're suddenly at peace with it all, and your next move is obvious. You have just enough time to feel the invigorating wind on your face and crack a smile as you perform your final somersault.

I'm not saying that everyone should quit their job and go on a bender. There are plenty of ways to start feeling the wind on your face, enjoying the views, and performing somersaults right now. All it requires is a subtle perspective shift. Stop seeing something like your job as a means to an end, but rather as a perfectly worthy end in and of itself. "My crummy job? How could *that* be a worthy end??" you might ask. How, indeed... Many would rapidly reject this idea without even considering investigating it on their own, instead opting to double down on their parachutes. Call it a "sunk cost fallacy" or a "mid-life crisis," but yacht number nine won't do anything for you if you can't enjoy the sea without the yacht.

You'd think people would try another game after their first parachute fails them, but there's always some new self-help guru swooping in with a hang glider to save you. They're very convincing in their pitch that the *real* problem is not trying hard enough, and that you must commit *even harder* to the "I can do things" habit. The problem with parachutes is that even when they fail, they still feel like they worked until that point. The self-help gurus are great, and the shiny new hang glider really feels like it works... until you look up. You're still betting it all on a salvation positioned just out of reach in a tomorrow that never arrives. Please remind me of the definition of "insanity." I'd tell you to spend your life somersaulting, but then you'd probably pursue parachutes made of somersaults.

When you drive that new sports car off the lot, you really think you've now got the improvement that you were chasing. Then when that runs its course, you think your problem is that you didn't get a *nice enough* sports car, so you double down on a nicer one. Again, this works for a while... until it doesn't. It feels like the cars are failing you, but the thing that keeps failing you is the thing you keep doubling down on: Game A. Since the cars feel like the problem, you decide to drop the materialistic collecting after encountering a guru who says that a spiritual awakening will allow you to *truly* become your highest self. Rinse and repeat.

The guru's pitch is convincing because it's what you want to hear. It allows the Game A player to keep up the charade and feel better for a few years. The fact that gurus seem to help so many people is exactly why I dislike them. Hang gliders annoy me *because* they work... until they don't. They simply draw out the crisis through the illusion of progress. The problem with the improvement game is you can *always* be better, so there will always be someone ready to sell you a better toy, career, love life, education, religion, philosophy, or worldview.

Call it tough love, but I'd rather tell you an uncomfortable truth than sell you a comfortable lie. The discomfort that someone feels after their parachute fails is the feeling of Game A collapsing around them. It's the storm before the calm. I say let it collapse. Let them wobble and wrestle with the realization that their parachute was a mirage. Then a new guru swoops in to prop it all back up and delay the inevitable collapse. The hang glider eliminates the discomfort and allows you to keep clinging to the habit, which you're obviously biased toward if it's a habit of yours. Game A will read this and think "the comfort zone is bad. Getting out of my comfort zone will save me." Any move made from this frame is still operating within the comfort zone of the habit.

When you visit a Swedish spa, you jump from hot pools to cold pools and back again. If you sit in the delightful warmth of a hot tub for too long, it becomes miserable. If someone only ever took cold showers and baths, then would it take courage for them to get in a hot tub? Playing Game A is like spending decades in the cushy comfort of the hot tub. At a certain point, you start to overheat and feel like something is wrong. Too much comfort can get pretty uncomfortable. Game B is the cold pool that few realize they're craving, and even fewer ever get immersed in. Some might dip their toes in the cold pool and say "no way!" Others might dive in for Game A reasons. Wim Hof recently popularized the use of ice baths, which has not surprisingly been adopted by the fitness community as another method of improvement. Classic hang glider. Many who believe that they're sitting in the cold pool of Game B are really just driving away from the spa.

The funny thing is that Game B actually provides an immense amount of comfort and stress relief, but only once you're on the other side of the discomfort felt during Game A's collapse. I'd also like to stress that some people *love* playing the improvement game. You can definitely play Game A for Game B reasons. If Game A is your somersault, then that's amazing. If it's your parachute, then it might be a good time for you to look up.

I can't make you see Game B in a lasting or meaningful way. The best I can do is give you brief windows to peek inside. Maybe your mind was blown by an anecdote or exercise in this book, and you had a taste of a mystical experience. Maybe you feel like you now have a strong conceptual understanding of Game B as a worldview. As wonderful as that would be, I feel like these breakthroughs can never be more than a shadow of a taste of what's really on offer when you find your own way to the buffet. I call this phenomenon "flashlight cranking." While I'm able to briefly enlighten through a form of state transference, the moment I stop is the moment you default back to your habits and conditioning. It's a fleeting form of fake Game B.

It never seems to stick when it comes from me, and appears to operate by the *Inception* (2010) rule that the idea must come from you. The best I seem to be able to produce in others is a form of legal hairline crack, which has a fascinating tendency to work itself bigger and bigger when left alone over time. I've had friends tell me:

> Remember that thing you said a year ago about [insert some flippant comment that I zero percent remember]? I haven't stopped thinking about it, and [they proceed to explain their revelations about a Game B insight I had explicitly tried to tell them dozens of times].

In this example, the insight didn't really come from me. My words just pointed them in the general direction. At the end of the day, you'll see it for yourself if and when you're meant to. You can only fall down this rabbit hole if you're looking for it on some level.

When someone falls down (literally or metaphorically) from a Game A perspective, they might think: "If I can only improve myself, then next time it won't hurt so much." When someone falls down from a Game B perspective, they might think: "Wow! What a ride!" When Game A comes in contact with Game B ideas, it says "that is the experience that I want to have. The next time I fall down, I should accept it and say to myself: 'Wow! What a ride!' Then I'll really get the most out of life." This is just another way of trying to improve, but is so camouflaged by complexity that it's difficult to recognize as Game A anymore.

When the Game B perspective reads the above, it recognizes that the Game-A-centred misunderstanding of Game B is still just a part of the ride. It also recognizes that bonafide Game B insights are also just a part of the ride. The Game B perspective sees that Game A and Game B are not actually different. They're just on different parts of the ride, and the ride is much bigger than first imagined. How big is it? I haven't got the slightest idea. Don't confuse "Game B sees that it's all a ride" with "Game B sees all of the ride."

You might be latching onto Game B because you think it's the answer you seek. You might keep reading because you want to figure it out. You might even think you've figured out that *this* is where it's at. This is still just repackaged Game A. Truly seeing Game B is the realization that despite seeing both sides now, you really don't know life at all.

J2. House of cards

It's better to destroy people's beliefs than to give them beliefs. I know it hurts, but it is The Way.

— Alan Watts

Is there anything that you confidently know for sure? Your knee-jerk reaction might be an obvious "yes." If so, you're probably looking from a zoomed in perspective, where each card representing a belief is supported by cards below it. The obvious question then becomes: What's supporting those cards? Zoom out enough, and you might see that your house of cards is built upon a quicksand foundation. Once I saw this structural flaw in my own house of cards, all it took was two little words to get the whole thing wobbling: Maybe not.

After having his own house of cards collapse, my brother arrived at the conclusion that the only claim he could confidently make was "there's something going on right now." Even then, this is assuming that we can trust our senses. We talk a lot about "concrete evidence," "objective reality," and "undeniable facts." But like… isn't every piece of data gathered in support of these objective facts collected from the subjective point of view of the researchers? The data is an account of what they saw. Can we trust their senses? Does a bunch of subjective perspectives add up to one objective perspective of capital T "Truth"?

I feel like we've lost sight of what science can and can't do. Science as a method of inquiry is excellent at predicting what's going to happen in given circumstances. There's a big difference between predicting what's going to happen next and claiming to know the way things are. Those kinds of claims about capital T "Truth" look more like religious dogma to me than a method of inquiry. If we were really advocates of inquiry, then we'd never stop inquiring about those things we claim to know. Science as a worldview looks rather unscientific to me.

Does the falling of a dropped stone prove the existence of gravity, or does gravity do a really good job of predicting the behavior of a dropped stone? Does the stone fall because of gravity, or does it fall because it does? Shouldn't we investigate this? The concept of "proof" seems like an excuse to stop inquiring, since the panel of experts has ruled that the evidence presented is good enough for them. I couldn't possibly prove that I've been to Mars, but you couldn't possibly prove that you've been to Earth. From where I'm sitting, the belief that the Earth is flat is no more absurd than the belief that the Earth is round. Both beliefs are 100% leaps of faith with the same amount of evidence to back them up: Zero. Consider the following exchange:

Student: The Earth is round.

Master: You're just saying that it is.

Student: But it is.

Master: Exactly.

You might contend that "saying it doesn't make it true," but don't we do this with everything else? There was a time when people said the Earth was flat, and for them it *really* was. You probably feel very strongly that it *really* is round, and that is precisely my point. If some extra-dimensional being thinks we're foolish for calling it round when it's clearly a splarg, then they'd be doing the same thing as us. Is an apple more "apple" than "snorkel"? You might call it a very poor snorkel. I might disagree. Is one of us objectively right?

Story Time: Swimming Lessons

Today is your son's first swimming lesson, so you pack him what you feel is an appropriate starter kit:

- Floaties/water wings to keep him afloat
- Goggles to help him see underwater
- A pair of quick drying swim trunks in his size

Your son comes home from his first class, drops his backpack on the counter, and you notice it has an odd shape. Opening it to examine its contents, you find:

- An inflated party balloon
- A magnifying glass
- An oversized bathrobe

"Where did these come from?" you ask.

"The instructor," he replies.

"What's he teaching you?"

"Swimming."

"How are you swimming with these?"
"I'm not sure what you're asking... In the water, silly."

The next class, you show up early to pick-up your son with the intention to give the instructor a piece of your mind.

Upon entering, you see several children dilly-dallying in the water. Your son is bobbing around with his balloon, and is looking through his magnifying glass. Upon closer inspection, you notice they're all wearing normal clothes.

The instructor is a hippy-looking loser. He's standing beside a box full of items that don't belong in a pool and is shouting "great work!" to your son, who has now picked up an oversized paintbrush and is flicking water at the walls. What the…

"Hey! What are you teaching these kids?" you demand.

"Swimming. Nice to meet you sir. Your son is one of my brightest stars," says the instructor with enthusiasm.

"You can't teach like this! That's not swimming," you insist.

"I appreciate your concern and would like to address it, but I don't know what you mean."

"You must be trolling me. You can't be that stupid. They're just flopping around. They aren't going anywhere!"

"How do you suppose I should teach them?"

"They should be doing drills and swimming in lines."

"I'm sorry, but I don't understand."

"Like this, you moron."

You strip down to your underwear and jump in the pool. The water gives you a brisk shock that is uncomfortable, but makes you forget some of your anger. You swim as fast as possible back and forth in the pool until you're completely out of breath. It feels like forever, but realistically the whole thing probably doesn't last more than a minute.

Exhausted and in a daze, you notice the entire class is watching you intently. "Let's all thank the nice man for that *spectacular* display of swimming," the instructor says. You can tell from the tone of his voice and the look on his face that he's both sincere and impressed. The class erupts with cheers, and your son has a huge smile on his face. You look down and see a giant paintbrush in your hands.

For some reason, Game A gives much more credit to Game B ideas when they're written down in a book, as if they're suddenly handed down from the gods. I suspect this stems from the fact that most people are ringwraiths, and already have a habit of worshiping words themselves as capital T "Truth." I can tell someone the same thing in person, and it's easy to dismiss it as some idiot's idea. And yet every word you've ever read in a book was some idiot's idea in the exact same way. I'm no theologian, but I'm pretty sure Jesus, Buddha, and Mohammed were just some idiot with an idea too. Jiddu Krishnamurti points out that thought creates the religious symbol, and then thought worships it, so thoughts are worshiping thoughts…

Everything you know is obstructing you from seeing that you don't know anything. As Terence McKenna observed, modern science's approach to the "how does it all work" game is to say "give us one free miracle, and we'll explain the rest," conveniently ignoring a pretty enormous elephant in the room. Even briefly glancing at this elephant causes a house of cards to wobble. The power of "I don't know" is a force to be reckoned with. You can't say with complete certainty that the world behind your head exists, or that the world from five seconds ago actually happened the way you think it did.

Whenever I'm blowing on someone's house of cards, they often presume that I'm advocating for nihilism. "You can say that nothing matters" will come up over and over, despite my never having said any such thing. As explored in the prior section, Game A repackages everything I say, and in this case hears "nihilism." What I'm trying to say is "let's get rid of some of this sauce so that you can actually taste the hot dog," but what they hear is "let's get rid of this hot dog. Who needs it anyway?" They think the sauce *is* the hot dog, because that's their daily experience of life. Therefore, removing the sauce is removing life itself, and is throwing out the baby with the bathwater from their perspective. The more knowledge we hold, the more knowledge holds us. According to Tyler Durden in Chuck Palahniuk's *Fight Club*, "the things you own end up owning you."

Exercise: The Edge of Self

Let's find the edge of ourselves.

a) Try and point to an edge between you and not you?

b) Can you think of anything inside of that boundary that you WOULD NOT instinctively recognize as yourself?

c) Can you think of anything outside of that boundary that you WOULD instinctively recognize as yourself?

d) Are you able to point to an edge that yields a NO answer to both (b) & (c)?

e) Hey you. Yeah, YOU. Do you recognize yourself in (e)?

The idea of reincarnation makes perfect sense from a Game B perspective. It's not that "me" will come back as something else. It's that you aren't actually "me" at all, and the thing that you really are is already all of the other things. You were simply playing the game of pretending that you were not "god" (whatever that is), so that when you rediscovered that you were, it would be that much more fun. Alan Watts refers to this as one big game of hide and seek: "You find out that the universe is a system that creeps up on itself and says 'Boo!', and then laughs at itself for jumping." Once the house of cards of "me" collapses, then what's left?

Exercise: The Death of Self

Scientists studying the strong bond experienced by twins have devised a pill that allows everyone taking it to share the same connection. During clinical trials, 20 randomly sampled subjects shared what they described as an intense connection, closer than what they felt with close friends or immediate family. All 20 of them described feeling as if they actually *were* each other.

a) What practical applications do you see for such a pill? To whom would you prescribe it?

b) Would you take this pill? Why or why not?

c) If you and I both took this pill, then who's writing or reading this book?

One of the things I find fascinating about Game B as a worldview is that it appears to be the opposite of a house of cards. It's an iron bunker that can't collapse. It may be a "perfect" worldview in this way, as nothing I throw at it can dent it. Perhaps this is because I'm trying to collapse a house of cards that has already collapsed. Building it up doesn't collapse it either, because it still just is what it is. As far as I can tell, it's the simplest possible worldview and the ultimate Occam's Razor: This. Even if it isn't this, then wouldn't that make it... this? We could call it "not this," but we'd still be attaching that label to this. Said another way: This is how it is now... and this is how it is now. When your worldview fully accounts for "maybe not," then it remains consistent and unshakable no matter what you encounter.

This is difficult to explain with language. I once thought of it like two bookends on a shelf. Even if you introduce something outside of the bookends, they immediately expand to contain everything neatly on the shelf. In this way, Game B actually contains all other games within it. It's more difficult to explain what Game B is compared to Game A because definition requires exclusion, and Game B includes all of it, including the exclusion. Game B is both 100% fluid and rock solid, unlike the rigid fragility of Game A, or the distinctive wobble of the Jungle. It's like an infinite reservoir that has no problem holding all of the water that the dam fails to contain when it inevitably breaks.

Even if you disproved or effectively maybe not'd the maybe not, then the system sort of just laughs. No amount of maybe nots piled on will cause an ounce of wobble from a Game B perspective, which provides the solid foundation that Game A craves and ultimately can't have down at its base. Maybe this grounding aspect of Game B can anchor you during a storm of wobble. Maybe not. If all of this nonsense has got you wobbling, then maybe you can find a sense of grounding in pointing out and naming the wobble. Maybe not. I'll shut up now.

J3. Running out of road

I believe that all roads lead to the same place, and that is wherever all roads lead to.

— Willie Nelson

It's usually easy to get someone to see that they're playing Game A. If they look closely, they'll also see the obvious flaws with that game. What people don't expect is the host of consequences that come from even considering dropping Game A. One of the biggest issues that arises is a perceived nihilism stemming from an inability to even fathom an alternative game. What would that look like? Life feels pretty meaningless when all of your meaning is tied up in improvement.

You might ask "what am I working toward if I can't improve?" I'd turn that question around and ask what you planned on doing with all that improvement you've accumulated. Do you wish to have your riches sealed in your tomb with you to guarantee safer passage to the afterlife? Perhaps you'd like a statue made in your likeness to immortalize your great accomplishments. The poem *Ozymandias* by Percy Shelley highlights the fatal weakness of all statues: The sands of time. As Roy Batty says in *Blade Runner* (1982), "all those moments will be lost in time, like tears in rain." Given enough time, even the most permanent structures will erode and crumble. If you're drowning in the despair of it all being washed away, Game B insights offer two potential life preservers in both your now experience and your legacy.

When it comes to your now experience, you might take comfort in the thought that you aren't dead yet, and today is always ripe for the seizing. Finding joy, purpose, or meaning in the present moment may not save you in the end, but it's a pretty great consolation prize if you ask me. A wise man doesn't spend his time fishing in tomorrow. He spends it fishing in a lake.

Story Time: Then What?

There's an old man who loves to fish, and does it every day. One day, a businessman joins him on his boat, and is blown away by his fishing ability. He urges the fisherman to start a business and convert the whole area into a large fishery, as he's convinced it would be wildly successful.

"What will I do once it's successful?" asks the fisherman.

"Retire and do whatever you want!" replies the businessman.

The fisherman calmly says: "I like to fish."

When it comes to your legacy, you might take comfort in the thought of breaking the chains of your limited body to transcend death itself. Your ancestors may be gone, but they're still in the painting. You are their walking legacy; they march on through you. You are their talking legacy; they echo through you. I remember walking home from yoga in the winter of 2019 and feeling like I wasn't walking at all. I was moving without any effort, and was instead being undeniably pushed by some force from behind. I imagined a long line of ghosts—my ancestors, and everything they ever did to get me to that point—pushing me forward. The question arose in my mind: "Who's pushing them?"

Upon telling my brother about this experience, he posed a question that blew my mind: "Who are you pushing?"

> And then I started to think, what if we're all in the painting everywhere? What if we're in the painting before we're born? What if we're in it after we die? And these colors that we keep adding... What if they just keep getting added on top of one another, until eventually we're not even different colors anymore; we're just one thing. One painting. [...] I think maybe that's the point of the whole thing. There's no dying. There's no you, or me, or them. It's just us. And this sloppy, wild, colorful, magical thing that has no beginning, it has no end... it's right here. I think it's us.
>
> *This Is Us* (2016)

You might find profound meaning in this relationship. I know I do. Everyone's Game B tends to have its own theme, and mine happens to be all about intertextuality. I tried not to define Game B too precisely earlier because *your* Game B will probably have its own distinct flavor, which I'd like to leave some space for. Yours might be about catharsis, reflection, playfulness, or something impossible to define with words. Mine has this strong sense of everything being "built in" to everything else, making it all intertwined and impossible to untangle.

Events that took place a thousand years ago are built into my experiences, which are built into events set to pass a thousand years from now. Said another way: Life is like a fully loaded YouTube video, and we're simply the dot steadily sliding along the bar at the bottom. Imagine a long chain of domino blocks. Each block is being pushed by the one behind it and is pushing the one in front of it. When you start looking at things in this way, it becomes easy to see how it's all linked and impossible to disentangle.

Look at a Van Gogh painting, and you can feel his gestures reaching through time to touch you. I find this phenomenon both incredibly magical and incredibly easy to miss. Every time I listen to a Bing Crosby song, I feel him rising from the grave to dance along my eardrums. Moreover, I feel like we're the stewards of his voice, should we wish to allow him to keep rising for future generations. Listen to a recorded concert performance of a song, and it might be easier to feel this sense of time traveling back to that moment. I can remember listening to an Elvis Presley song recently and feeling like I was physically in the studio with him at the time of its recording. At that moment, I had no sense that he was "dead" or "gone." He was right there in the room with me.

Spend some time with these ideas, and you might see how the connections flow in both directions. My experiences are equally built into events that took place a thousand years ago. When you look at a Van Gogh painting, you're equally reaching back through time to touch him. Hit rewind on the YouTube video, and suddenly it looks like your enthusiasm for his painting inspires its creation in the first place. We're all time travelers, and it's all built in.

The simple fact of our mortality can either obliterate your sense of meaning and spiral you into nihilism, or become an infinite source of profound meaning. As profound as any new meaning acquired by playing Game B or even returning to Game A may be, you may wrestle with the realization that the improvement ride and the performance ride share a trait in common with all rides: They end. Whether you're stacking up your house of cards or marveling at its collapse, we're all going to the end of the line.

If the aforementioned life preservers can address the existential wobble that can arise from the prospect of dropping Game A, then should we all cling to them and hold on for dear life? Can we ride them into salvation and out of the Jungle? A conceptual life preserver won't save you. Concepts are about as useful at solving the problem of concepts as a net is for catching water. A conceptual life preserver won't save you from the Jungle because a conceptual life preserver *is* the Jungle. It will likely only perpetuate the wobble in the long run, despite the momentary salvation it seems to provide. A concept can't save you from the prison of concepts. It's just another brick you've laid in the wall you wish to knock down.

J4. Grasping at smoke

If you have to ask what jazz is, you'll never know.

— Louis Armstrong

Have you ever had an experience so perfect that you found yourself wishing you could bottle it and hold onto it forever? We previously discussed how boxing experiences into concepts interferes with the experiences themselves, and how this compulsion turns people into ringwraiths. Anyone who manages to avoid this compulsion long enough to have a mystical or 10/10 experience then runs into a different form of boxing: Grasping at smoke. This variation on boxing occurs when we recognize that we've got the thing we want, which presents a new problem: We might lose it. Now we try to cling on to this non-ringwraith experience, but clinging on is a total ringwraith move.

We try to box or bottle these magic moments for safekeeping, but these moments are magical *because* they're fleeting. To bottle smoke is to de-smokify it. Just like with the labeling form of boxing, grasping for it kills it. A parent whips out their phone to capture their child doing something magical, only for the presence of the recording phone to alter the mood in the room into something distinctly less magical. At the end of "Colors of the Wind" in Disney's *Pocahontas* (1995), our title character hands John Smith a pile of dirt, which immediately starts to slip through his fingers. Try to hold onto it, and you'll find it slipping away from you. Try to let go of it, and you'll find it in your hands.

Watch a toddler experience a spontaneous magic moment, and their response is often to try and immediately recreate it. They begin a futile process of trying to force spontaneity. But trying to create it is not what created it in the first place. Their recreated moment can only ever be a shadow of the spontaneous one. They'll soon tire of these shadow moments, which run their course and are less and less potent, until they drop the forcing altogether and BOOM: A new spontaneous moment strikes. Cue the forced recreation all over again.

In *The Nightmare Before Christmas*, Jack Skellington clearly has a 10/10 experience in Christmas Town, then returns to Halloween Town and struggles to explain it to everyone, including himself. He knows it's special and deeply meaningful, but can't pin down why. He locks himself away, studying books and artifacts in an attempt to figure out the secret of this Christmas thing he just experienced: "Here in an instant, gone in a flash!" Was it something in the composition of the texts or the trinkets? No. Those items are simply the sauce that complemented the feast, and can never stand-in as the feast itself. His tortured mind offers an excellent example of what grasping at smoke in the Jungle looks like:

> Christmas time is buzzing in my skull
> Will it let me be? I cannot tell
> There's so many things I cannot grasp
> When I think I've got it, then at last
> Through my bony fingers it does slip
> Like a snowflake in a fiery grip
>
> "Jack's Obsession" (Danny Elfman)

Jack even realizes that the thing he's trying to bottle is "like music drifting in the air: Invisible, but everywhere." However, he still makes the same mistake as the toddler, in trying to recreate the ephemeral experience. Was that how he "got it" in the first place? He clearly stumbled into it by accident, and is now trying to plan his way into spontaneity. If he really wanted to recreate the magic, he should return to the aimless stumbling that set the conditions from which it bloomed last time. Even then, there'd be a planned aspect to it, which wasn't there in the lead up to the experience he's trying to bottle.

In the viral YouTube video "Yosemitebear Mountain Double Rainbow 1-8-10," we see how a right brain sensory overload eclipses the usual left brain cognitions. When faced with such awe-inspiring imagery, Paul "Bear" Vasquez struggles to formulate words, resorting to shouting primal noises as he rides a cathartic rush of endorphins and is overwhelmed with emotion. He says "it's too much," as he oscillates between laughing and crying uncontrollably. The left brain elements are there (the fact that he started recording it at all suggests a grasping at smoke ringwraith habit), but there's a clear moment when he is totally overwhelmed and the monkey mind short circuits.

Once the monkey mind is done booting back up, you see him immediately try to make sense of the experience, asking desperately: "What does it mean??" He cries out and begs for an answer in a language that he can understand: "Tell me what it means!" From my point of view, it's painfully obvious what it means, but it's packaged in a language the left brain can't understand. It's the same language that Pierre Trudeau failed to see any meaningful answer in when gazing up at the snowflakes. Go watch the video and see if you can hear it.

Vasquez is clearly having a life-defining 10/10 experience, and is looking for someone or something else to explain it to him. Who could possibly be a more qualified expert on this experience than him? The message was more than adequate as an explanation from a right brain frame, but it falls woefully short of satisfying his saucy conceptual questions. People fortunate enough to have these kinds of mystical experiences often spend the rest of their days searching for some meaning beyond the experience itself. They tend not to find anything because they're fish looking for water.

The double rainbow video seems to have gone viral because viewers enjoy mocking his dramatic reaction to what looks like a couple of boring rainbows. They'd probably mock Moses for making a big deal out of a boring bush. While they find it incredibly funny, I find it incredibly moving. If you're still not seeing any profound message, then try taking it at face value. The experienced world is not some riddle that needs solving. Alan Watts says "the sound of the rain needs no translation," which you're probably already trying to decode.

I'll concede that we're able to bottle the magic in a very limited way… but also not really. Plenty of pictures, paintings, and poems have managed to capture an image, memory, or feeling that we recognize as a piece of the fleeting moment it evokes. We may even recognize the video as no different than the moment itself. I mean, there it is, after all. If I watch the video of the moment and am deeply moved by it, then the moment has effectively been bottled. Right? My gut says no, because the video itself is a signpost pointing at the moment, and therefore can't stand in for the moment itself. Said another way: It's not a video of a video. Each time I'm moved by that video is a new fleeting moment; another plume of smoke comes and goes.

After reading "The Unsipped Beers" and "The Unsipped Beers Part II" in the above sections, you might now think that being Morgan is where it's at, since that's literally what's written. While you wouldn't be wrong (Morgan *is* living the dream), you'd be missing the nuance that Morgan wants to experience Taylor and Alex's unsipped beers, so

Morgan does exactly that. Wanting to be Morgan to "be Morgan" is absurd, since all of the value Morgan experiences comes from the experience itself (and not from 'the experience itself'). Morgan isn't wishing to experience the unsipped beers while they experience the unsipped beers. This kind of thinking is the same ringwraith habit displayed by Taylor and Alex in not sipping their beers, but in a much more confusing and tangled way. It convinces you that you actually are sipping it, even though you aren't receiving any of the benefits of sipping it. I probably lost you three sentences ago. Me trying to write this coherently and you trying to understand it are precisely the kinds of paths that lead directly into the Jungle, so forget all of the above and go sip your beer (whatever that looks like for you).

While a toddler will try to grasp at smoke, they won't become seriously tangled in the Jungle yet because they're so much closer to level one. At level 645, you're so lost in the sauce that you think the only way out is by adding sauce. This approach doesn't work, so you think that removing sauce is the answer. But now you're adding "removing sauce" sauce, and you're still trying to sauce your way out of sauce. Good luck.

J5. But how? (still the habit)

Grown-ups never understand anything by themselves, and it is tiresome for children to be always and forever explaining things to them.

— Antoine de Saint-Exupéry (The Little Prince)

People in the wellness and spiritual fields talk a lot about meditation and mindfulness as a means of quieting the monkey mind. While I don't deny that these practices can be useful tools, I see one giant problem with them: They're a very highbrow version of the habit (I can do things), which are predicated on doing your way into being. It's still just a clever repackaging of the improvement game, which leads many into even more frustration when the tools don't end up working for them. Jiddu Krishnamurti says "when you fight a habit, you give life to that habit, and the fighting becomes another habit."

I constantly hear people say "I can't meditate. I sit for five minutes, but then I get distracted and give up." Now they feel even worse about themselves for "failing" at the improvement game, reinforcing their worldview that they're not good enough to meditate. While guided and technique-based mediation can be great entry points into the practice, they suffer from the rigidity of instructions. It places a burden of performance on the doer, which can obviously lead to performance anxiety. I'd wager that taking a shower or going for a walk is much more meditative for the average person than meditation, since the shower and the walk don't come with all of the associated expectations of results and pressures to perform.

I once had a student tell me that when she visualizes the day ahead in the morning, she's overwhelmed by all of the things she has to do, which completely stifles her productivity. However, she said that if she just gets up and goes without thinking, then she has no problem tackling everything on her to-do list. In this case, a passive or autopilot mindset can actually increase productivity by completely removing the burden of performance. The trap the Jungle will set here is that now you think that "just get up and go" is the instruction to follow or do in order to realize increased productivity. But she wasn't saying that at all.

The same student noted that "in society, there's this expectation that everything needs to be done," and said her understanding of meditation was a form of "watching the cars go by." I asked whether something she considered more of an activity than meditation, like going to write an exam, could also be just as passive as watching the cars go by. She countered that you still need to write the exam: "You need to think about your answers." I asked: "Where are those thoughts coming from?" She replied: "Your brain..." I asked: "Aren't *those* thoughts passing by too? How are they any different than the thoughts that pass by when you meditate?" I can watch myself think of the answers, write them down, and hand in the exam from a 100% passive lens, and my experience is 100% congruent with that perspective. It just happened, like a car passing by.

In *The Dark Knight*, the Joker tries to explain the lack of method behind his madness. Accused of being a man with a plan, he counters that "I'm a dog chasing cars. I wouldn't know what to do with one if I caught it. You know? I just... do... things." I'm not saying we need to become supervillains to kick the "I can do things" habit. I'm saying that I don't have a plan for how to end this paragraph. I'm just ending it.

I remember playing a small tabletop basketball game with a coworker, and she was struggling to make a basket. She was on a very long string of misses, when I looked at her and said "just do it." Before she could even think about it, she scored a perfect shot. The ultimate version of getting out of your own way is for the "you" to dissolve entirely. You can't be in your own way if there's no "you" to be in your way. At that moment, there was no "she" doing it. "Just do it" happened. Then her monkey mind kicked in and said "ohh, *just do it* is the method I need to do." Needless to say, she went right back to missing again and again.

Everyone knows the first rule of holes: Stop digging. One of the best ways to see what I'm pointing at is to run out of road (or if you're digging, to reach bedrock or fall through the bottom). The sticky thing about the Jungle is that it's very difficult to run out of road as long as you keep laying new road in front of you. It never ceases to amaze me how much road people are capable of laying in front of them; many never stop. As mentioned before, a terminal illness diagnosis is a great way to run out of road. However, people with experience in palliative care tell me that some never give up the ghost, and go out kicking and screaming. They never manage to let go of their imagined parachute and treat themselves to a somersault.

We accept that a definition including the word being defined is a problematic definition. Yet we try to explain away labels with more labels. It's like labeling a label, then smacking it on a label and thinking you're moving beyond labels, when all you've done is add *more* labels to the label pile. Cue cognitive dissonance, since your conceptual location is at odds with your experienced location: Drowning in sauce. Toe says "labels are a disaster." Alan Watts says "you're trying to straighten out a wiggly world and no wonder you're in trouble."

Maybe we could make peace with the wiggly nature of the world. But how?? It's less about the *act* of allowing, and more about the *art* of allowing. Read the following sentence with and then without the bolded words: I am **trying to do** something the "right" or "perfect" way. A wise Jedi master once said "do… or do not. There is no try." Consider another example: I am **trying to be** a better person. Notice how the trying looks more like an obstacle in the way of what you want than a means of attaining it. Jiddu Krishnamurti observes: "It is strange how we want freedom and do everything to enslave ourselves."

We could say that a method isn't required for an artist to paint a piece. A friend of mine was looking at a half-done piece, when I said "I'm going to add a couple of figures down here," pointing at a spot on the canvas. This statement broke his brain, since he was locked up with analysis paralysis at the time. He immediately asked "how are you going to do that?" I almost didn't understand the question, and replied: "I don't know. I'm just gonna do it, and however it looks is how it's supposed to look." He was very suspicious and didn't understand. He stared at the spot, picked up my palette knife, and started gesturing in the air, trying to imagine how he might add the figures. It seemed like an impossible gap for him to bridge without a method to rely on.

Story Time: The Two Buddhas

One Buddha says to another: "You're the best." The other Buddha thinks: "Wow. The best person just gave me a free lesson on how to be more like them. Easy for them to say… They're the best and I'm not."

Plenty of people want to be a buddha. The same people would tell you they've got no idea what it feels like to be a buddha… So how can they know they want that? Buddha says he sees everyone as buddhas (you're already there). People hear "seeing everyone as buddhas is the secret to becoming a buddha" (the key to improvement). If what he meant was the latter, he would've said the latter. Take him at face value.

Spoiler for *Kung Fu Panda* (2008) follows (go watch it first!). Notice how the Dragon Scroll, which contains the secret to "limitless power," is blank. Po later translates this to his personal context as "there is no secret ingredient." While it works for the purpose of the film, Po is not taking the scroll at face value. The scroll doesn't say "there is no secret ingredient." If Master Oogway meant that, he obviously would have written that, or some version of that like "the secret to limitless power is to believe in yourself." He didn't write that. He didn't write anything. It's just blank. *That* is the secret. You may now interpret this to mean that "blank scroll" is the secret, but you're still not taking him at face value. Oogway didn't draw a picture of a blank scroll on the scroll. He chose to write "   " for a reason. Take him at face value. It turns out we've all got Master Oogway's wisdom tattooed on our forehead.

Story Time: The Tricky Teacher

> Today is your first day in Ms. Derek's logic class. You've been warned that she's a trickster, and nothing is ever as it seems with her lessons. Your guard is up and you're prepared for the worst. She tells you there will be an early test next week, but assures you that it will be a breeze if you simply study the answer key she hands you a copy of. "Nice try, Ms. Derek," you think to yourself, as the voices of your older friends echo in your head: "Don't buy it."
>
> Instead, you spend your week burning the midnight oil. You manage to read everything in the syllabus, cross reference it with other editions, and even consult peripheral sources at the

library. By the end of the week, you fancy yourself a historical, theoretical, and applied expert on the curriculum. There's nothing she can throw at you that you haven't carefully studied.

The day of the test arrives, and you sit confidently sharpening your pencils (you made sure to bring two spares, just in case). She hands you the test and prompts you to begin. You glance at the questions, but there's just one problem: They aren't questions. The writing, if you can even call it that, appears to be some kind of cryptic code you've never seen. If only you had the answer key she gave you, which you never even looked at. Still, you try your best to outsmart the test by applying all of the knowledge you acquired in the past week.

Wouldn't it be nice if we could skip to the end of the improvement game? As far as I can tell, skipping to the end isn't just the fastest way to be better... it's the only way. This looks like cheating from Game A's perspective, which views picking up your piece and placing it at the finish as irresponsible, lazy, and a threat to honest progress. And yet, the only way to get there is to get there. You can't cross a finish line from a step behind it. You're either behind it or beyond it, and as long as you're behind it, then you aren't where you want to be. Alan Watts says "the reason you want to be better is the reason why you aren't."

If the goal of the improvement game is to be better, then tell yourself that "I *am* better, and this is what that looks like." Say it enough, and you might start believing it. "I *will* be better" is a statement that you aren't better, and you'll remain behind the finish line for as long as you keep saying it. Those who keep their better selves stuck in the future tend to see themselves as boldly powering forward, because "success is a moving target." From my perspective, I see someone so focused on spinning their hamster wheel that they're blind to the fact that one baby step to the side gets them exactly what they want.

Neo: What are you trying to tell me? That I can dodge bullets?

Morpheus: No, Neo. I'm trying to tell you that when you're ready, you won't have to.

The Matrix

J6. The tough pill to swallow

I didn't say it would be easy.

— Morpheus (The Matrix)

In the transition from Game A to Game B, things are likely to get bitter before they get better. It does get better on the other end of the rabbit hole, but some of the insights along the way can be pretty jarring when you've still got one foot in Game A. That said, there's likely some comfort to be found in knowing that this ride has some scary parts before they jump out at you. Not all surprises are fun surprises.

Am I being overly dramatic? Maybe. But I can't physically hold your hand right now, so this is the next best thing. When the mind is spooked by the wobble of a collapsing house of cards, it tends to evade with an impressive display of mental gymnastics. Look inward with total honesty, and you'll probably see some impressively inconsistent picking and choosing going on. Animals don't like to be threatened, and neither do the deeply held beliefs we've been clinging to for decades. Human nature in three words: "This is different." We're capable of justifying some pretty horrible treatment of others under that banner. We also use it to justify some pretty horrible treatment of ourselves. The next time you hear those words used in the context of fear, rearrange them into a sincere question: Is this different?

Someone might be finally opening up to the idea that everyone is always the best version of themselves... until they realize that everyone means *everyone*, and there have been some pretty unsavory people.

How could *they* possibly be the best version of themselves? It takes courage to ask a question like that, and can be downright terrifying to investigate, so proceed with caution.

> The Guest House
> by Rumi
>
> This being human is a guest house.
> Every morning a new arrival.
>
> A joy, a depression, a meanness,
> some momentary awareness comes
> as an unexpected visitor.
>
> Welcome and entertain them all!
> Even if they are a crowd of sorrows,
> who violently sweep your house
> empty of its furniture,
> still, treat each guest honorably.
> He may be clearing you out
> for some new delight.
>
> The dark thought, the shame, the malice.
> meet them at the door laughing and invite them in.
>
> Be grateful for whatever comes.
> because each has been sent
> as a guide from beyond.

It's a difficult pill to swallow, but you don't need to take it. I'm not here to force anything on you. All I'm doing is showing you the different games available to you. If you want to forget all of this and go back to playing Game A your hardest, then I think you should play it to the hilt. Simply being aware of Game A and choosing to play it looks to me like you're playing it for Game B reasons, which will almost certainly provide many insights and benefits that you'd never see from blindly playing it. If you don't have the stomach for this, then you're still the best version of yourself in my book. If you aren't the best version of yourself in your book, then you're still the best version of yourself in my book. I can even confirm it, since it's literally in my book.

Not only have I observed an unsurprising revolt against the notion that some infamous people are the best versions of themselves, but I've also noticed a surprising visceral pushback against the notion that you're the best version of yourself. For some reason, one of the most egregious insults to someone locked in Game A is that they're good enough. I suppose this is because their entire life is staked on the opposite being true. And since their life is staked on it, Game A does not go gentle into that good night. If there's no more room for improvement, then we must accept that demon in the mirror.

It sounds absurd, but I've seen people violently lash out against the idea that they're good enough. I've seen close friendships end over the suggestion even being raised. I could be way off base, but I'm fairly confident that Jesus was pushing a similar message, and was crucified for the way Game B is perceived from Game A's perspective. The message "you're good enough" is blasphemy of the highest order to someone who needs to improve in order to be saved. It's a threat to their very salvation, and can't be tolerated. Socrates was killed for corrupting the minds of the youth and speaking against the gods. Preaching that "I know nothing" is corrupting young minds that the state is invested in educating and speaking against the gods of "knowledge" that we've been raised to worship. It sounds like wisdom to me, but I can see how power structures aren't exactly warm to it.

These discussions can get dicey, as Game A tends to shame Game B for ethical, practical, and spiritual reasons. It doesn't surprise me that the improvement game claims to be a better game because it literally is the better game by definition. If "better" is your North Star, then that's actually a reasonable position to hold. I'll gladly give up the moral high ground, but where does that get us?

I realize that I'm being extra evasive right now. If you ever see what I mean, then you'll understand why I'm beating around this burning bush. If you understand, then I'm preaching to the choir. If you don't, then I'm just stoking the fires of "white must win over black" (and they're already white-hot). Rather than be baited into some seemingly reprehensible soundbite that will be touted as the grounds for burning all of my books, I'm putting on my politician hat and deflecting with my usual stock soundbite on this subject: I'll leave you to draw your own conclusions on that.

The Jungle summary

The Jungle comes out of a problem with the way we think. As far as I can tell, conversation has two vital functions:

- The experience or act of the sharing itself (which boils down to "I see you," and which language does very well). For example, "liking" someone's picture on social media.
- The transference of experiences or ideas.

I'd like to address a problem with the second function. When communicating with ourselves, we need not encode the message into words, and therefore can simply access it directly. I can think about a memory or a very specific shade of green without ever needing to explain it to myself. I simply experience that memory or that color.

Any experience or idea that one would like to transfer to another must be encoded in some form. The most common way to encode these messages is with words. Although we're exchanging words, the message being discussed is, in fact, not words. Therefore, if the receiver is to have any inkling of what the speaker is saying, they must share experiences or ideas that the words can relate to.

The words simply act as signposts pointing in the direction of the message, and cannot stand-in for the message itself. This becomes obvious when discussing something with someone who doesn't know a given word or has no real world experience with that word. What do we do when someone asks what a word means? We search for shared experience, or we show them if possible.

If someone asks "what does 'crustacean' mean?", then you might say: "It's a sea creature." If they ask "what's a sea creature?", then you might say: "It's a type of animal" (looking for broader and less accurate shared experience). We begin to see how the word "animal" does a pretty poor job of representing a crustacean. If accuracy was the aim, then we'd be better off showing the confused party a picture of a crustacean, or better yet handing them a live one.

Sharing certain messages calls for using words as a more obvious signpost pointing more directly toward the intended experience or idea. For example, "400 meters up that path is a magnificent waterfall" is a collection of words that doesn't transfer the experience that the speaker wishes to share, but describes how the receiver could directly access it. This type of communication transmits more accurately and therefore helps to transmit esoteric experiences and messages with small degrees of shared experience between the communicating parties.

The problem is that we seem to have forgotten that words have this limitation. They only have value insofar as they relate to *actual* experiences or ideas. Having forgotten this, we can't help but misunderstand the vast majority of what people say to us (and even what we say to ourselves). In our culture, the words themselves are more important, and almost invariably get mistaken for the experience or idea the speaker wished to share. Most of us would rather write down "400 meters up that path is a magnificent waterfall" and carry that note around with us in our pocket than actually follow the path and experience the waterfall, which can't be pocketed.

There's a good chance that the saying "stop and smell the roses" resonates with you. Perhaps you have it saved in a list of favorite quotes on your phone, and you repeat it as a mantrum, or you give it as advice to others. I challenge you: When was the last time you repeated those words, then searched out flowers and pushed your face into them? To repeat, commit to memory, or carry around the collection of words "stop and smell the roses" has the exact opposite meaning that the words are meant to represent.

Or perhaps you're more spiritual and you identify with "let go," "just watch," "don't force," "let it happen," "float like a cloud," "flow like water," "give up attachment," "stop grasping," "turn the other cheek," "sip the beer," "just do it," etc… In every case, these words represent an experience that isn't words at all. "Let go" doesn't mean the words "let go." No matter how many times one repeats it, reads it, carries it around, or tattoos it on their body, they'll never know what the Buddha was talking about until they take a minute and actually *let go*.

Unfortunately, we're so used to packaging and carrying words around with us that "just take a minute and actually *let go*" will almost certainly become the new collection of words that we repeat and carry with us. This collection once again undermines—or even blocks—the message the words hoped to deliver. This habit of trying to collect and carry around the right words, all the while leaving the beer sitting on the table unsipped, is the source of the Jungle.

The next time you're having a conversation with a friend, take a minute and *join them*, as close as you can, in the actual experiences or ideas they're trying to share. Spend too much time focusing on the signposts themselves, and you'll never see what they're pointing at.

J7. The way out

Wax on. Wax off.

— Mr. Miyagi (The Karate Kid)

While the rides at amusement parks tend to be amusing, the rides experienced when lost in a spiritual crisis tend to be rocky and unpleasant. Someone in the Jungle will often be perfectly able to see the various rides, but will want to get off of their current ride. They might even see how they're simply on the "I want off the ride" part of the ride, which will really get them wobbling. How do you get off of *that* ride?? Rest assured, it can be done. Let me rephrase: It can *happen*. We've already established that conceptual life preservers won't save you from concepts, which begs the question: "Where is the way out of the Jungle?" Perhaps a better question is not where, but *how*?

From my perspective, the type of power at play here has the same sort of existence as a menu: Seemingly permanent, graspable, and full of promise, but ultimately non-satiating and frustrating. I'm pointing you toward a type of power that has the same sort of existence as a meal: Ungraspable, but ultimately satiating. Like in a restaurant, the waiter takes back the menu before they deliver the meal. Giving up the menu is the hardest step to take, and requires the most courage. Most of us would rather have the guaranteed comfort of one more suck on the existential pacifier than the adventure and thrill of embracing the unknown. Ironically, the same person clinging to the menu will idealize mythic heroes who must leave home to go on their journey or binge watch motivational videos about the pitfalls of the comfort zone.

Imagine clinging to the menu and wishing for the meal to arrive at the same time. Cue cognitive dissonance.

Presumably, you found the courage to give up your pacifier before and can do it again. It sounds easy enough to give up the menu, but there's a major wrinkle in this process: Anyone trying to give up the menu is now likely clinging to the menu of "giving up the menu," and is so deep in menus of menus that they wouldn't even recognize a meal if it was sitting in front of them. When this happens, all I see is someone digging a hole and genuinely having no idea how to stop. Knowing the first rule of holes, I tell them to stop digging, but now they go digging for *that*.

We've previously touched on this problem of trying to sauce your way out of sauce, or use concepts to move beyond concepts. I can tell someone over and over that the way out of the Jungle is to "wax off" the concepts that have been piling up, but "wax off" is just another concept they'll add to their pile. Maybe they practice daily meditation to clear their mind of all those concepts piling up, and believe they're perfectly following the signs out of the Jungle. From their perspective, they see wax on, wax off, wax on, wax off, and don't understand why it isn't working. From my perspective, I see wax on, wax on, wax on, wax on, and it's obvious why it isn't working. Ultimately, to get it is to get that you don't get it. In realizing that you can't make a perfect painting, you realize that you're painting perfectly.

Suppose I told someone stuck in the Jungle the following: "There's no step you can take to move closer to here. You can't talk your way into silence. You can't plan your way into spontaneity." Now suppose they understood my words and the problem I'm highlighting, but still asked me for the method: "How *does* one be spontaneous?" How should I answer? We're both caught in a trap set by the question. To engage with the question at all is to feel the trap's teeth sinking in. Is the way out therefore not to pose such questions? Someone in the Jungle will ask "how do I avoid these questions?" The trap bites down harder.

Perhaps we could use the habit of "I can do things" against the perpetual doer, and let them run out of road on their own. Rather than pointing the way out of the Jungle, we could direct them deeper inside: "You're not planning enough. Plan *harder*, and then you'll become spontaneous." Once the peak of their efforts reveals the pointlessness of trying at all, they'll finally stop setting the trap, rather than trying to "stop setting the trap." They'll immediately see the folly of their predicament, and likely have a good laugh at the absurdity of it all: "*That* was the way out all along? Of course it was."

As I said before, one doesn't do their way out of the Jungle. It just happens, either because they've realized the futility of their enormous efforts to exit, or they've simply been distracted long enough to stop laying their own traps. In this way, the scale of the problem of exiting is as big or small as you make it. For some, it's like climbing Mount Everest, and can take years of intense cognitive wrestling. For others, it's as easy as stepping over an ant hill, and can be skipped in an instant.

Am I saying avoiding the Jungle is where it's at? Not at all. That would be another version of "white must win over black." I've come in and out of the Jungle several times over the past few years, without any obvious patterns as to why. Some of my stays were longer than others, but I never saw it as some existential problem that needed to be solved for my improvement. I like to remind myself that I enter and exit the Jungle precisely when I'm supposed to. Committing to that belief allows me to find myself inside some days and outside others, without ever feeling the really intense wobble that comes from fighting the trap. Your mileage may vary.

The Jungle is nothing more than a cognitive phenomenon, and the way out is simply to drop cognitions. However, all approaches, methods, and strategies to do so are also cognitions, which perpetuate the cycle. Cognitions are so seductive that they'll twist total non-cognitive artifacts like "   " or [pink flower emoji] into cognitive idols to strive for. If you can't beat them, join them. Feed the beast what it craves, until it dismantles itself from a cognitive overload and dissolves the Jungle entirely. Easier said than *done*.

The Thing

Despite having no knowledge of spirituality or Taoism, I arrived at my own version of the concept of the Tao in early 2019: The Thing. When I later learned of the Tao, I wasn't surprised to see that it was effectively the same idea, because it's such an obvious conclusion to land on when thinking through existential problems. As far as I can tell, it's the only possible conclusion: This. Posed as a question: Show me something other than what is?

If it gets confusing in the next pages, refer back to this flow chart:

Super official flow chart for determining whether or not something is the Thing

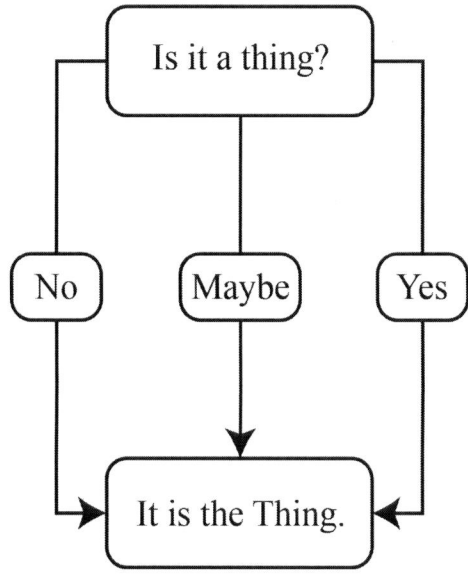

It's difficult to remember exactly how the idea initially presented itself, but it likely stemmed from seeing intensely profound meaning in counterintuitive subjects. I spent many hours awake at night working through the conceptual problems of existence. I was committed to figuring it all out, and it really felt like I was making solid progress. The real breakthrough came when I noticed that each separate solution I was arriving at seemed to point in the exact same direction: This.

"That's the Thing!" I would tell myself, followed by an immediate follow-up question: "How could *that* be the Thing?" "*That*'s the Thing!" I'd tell myself again, "because of course it is." How else could you get *that*? When you begin to take things at face value, it becomes obvious how they, too, are the Thing. Explaining it another way might look something like this: Something existing for the sake of itself (sort of the way you do). So maybe it's *always* the Thing, even when it isn't. It not being the Thing would *definitely* be the Thing, because of course it would. Classic Thing move. When in doubt, check the flow chart.

Let's consider the Thing from a Game A perspective: "This isn't the Thing. I must destroy this in order to move toward Not This." The problem here is that someone playing this game can make all sorts of moves that really give them the sense that they're progressing toward Not This. However, the end result is always the same: This. Their entire life is one big exercise in futility, where you feel constant progress but never reach the goal. It's like walking on a treadmill toward a finish line you can see but can't cross. If Jesus says "This is okay," and you're absolutely not okay with This, then what can you do? You can crucify Jesus and feel like you've destroyed this symbolic ambassador of This, but where does that get you? The end result is still This, because of course it is. This is the Thing. Not surprisingly, many people have no idea what I mean by Game B, but can easily recognize Game A and get on board with a goal of "Not This."

Let's consider the Thing from a Game B perspective: "Wow. This is clearly the Thing, and it's the Thingiest Thing it could be." This way of viewing This fosters much stronger engagement with This, since you aren't constantly trying to avoid or spin out of This. Stronger engagement creates the space for higher highs and lower lows, broadening your yin yang range. There's nothing to "do" except soak up the infinite perfection of the show you're being treated to. Writing this right now is kind of boring and oddly quiet, which I never would've noticed if I wasn't engaged with This. A boring and oddly quiet show is definitely the Thing. No matter what you're feeling at the moment, This is the Thing, because of course it is. Nothing the world throws at you can knock you out of This, because the world can only throw more This at you. This is happening right now, even when you don't like the way it looks. *This* is where it's at.

It seems like everyone is always saying some version of "This is where it's at," but what they really mean is "This will save me." Then everyone is constantly arguing about who has the fairest parachute of all. If you really had confidence that "This is where it's at," then you wouldn't need to convince anyone. Everyone is seeking external confirmation of their parachute, knowing in their heart of hearts that there's something wrong with it. But the person you seek confirmation from has the same problem. Good luck finding certainty in uncertainty.

All this from the guy trying to impose his ideas on you enough to put them in a book. That's rich. In my defense, I've tried very hard not to imply anywhere in this book that "This is where it's at" in some absolute parachute source of salvation kind of way. I don't say anything with that level of certainty (not even this statement). If anything, this is a book about leaving some space in your mind for This to be where it's at, no matter what This looks like. Am I saying that the sentence before this one is where it's at? Sure, but only insofar as it serves as the current form of This, which is all there ever is. So if it *is* where it's at, then it is, and if it *isn't* where it's at, then it isn't. Simple, right?

Is Game A where it's at? Sure. Is Game B where it's at? Sure. Is Game C where it's at? Wait… Game C is a thing?? Of course it is. It's *the* Thing. When in doubt, check the flow chart.

Game C

We've established a framework with (hopefully) clear definitions of a Game A and a Game B, and even some (almost certainly) murkier definitions of a Jungle and a Thing. I've danced long enough around a question likely bothering some of you: Is there a Game C? If so, then what's *that* game about?

The short answer is sure. Why not? A Game C (or X, Y, Z, Splarg, etc.) is any game not easily recognizable as being motivated by typical Game A or Game B pursuits. Consider someone who goes on a hunger strike, not to improve the world (typical Game A pursuit), and not to experience the hunger strike ride (typical Game B pursuit), but because their favorite color is blue. Now, you might say this non sequitur makes no sense. Does it objectively make no sense, or does it make no sense from your perspective? Consider whether you may be trying to apply your rules to an entirely other game, which has its own set of rules that don't interface well with yours. As I said previously: Basketball looks pretty absurd from the point of view of baseball rules. If you thought basketball and baseball were the only two sports in town, would you even recognize something like cheese rolling as a sport?

Exercise: One Weird Week

Let's get weird for a week.

DAY 1: Be liquid. Now go about your day as liquid.

DAY 2: Be them. Now go about your day as them.

DAY 3: Be love. Now go about your day as love.

DAY 4: Be bricks. Now go about your day as bricks.

DAY 5: Be 5. Now go about your day as 5.

DAY 6: Be vvvvv. Now go about your day as vvvvv.

DAY 7: Be be. Be be be be be be be be.

The "hunger strike blue" game is almost certainly confounding from the perspective of someone playing the improvement game. The improvement game player might have a sense that the "hunger strike blue" player is playing an entirely other game, but they'll most likely view them as someone playing Game A very poorly (and will likely offer to help them improve). This example likely seems absurd to you because you aren't playing that particular Game C, and haven't tried it. Remember that Game B looks equally absurd when viewed from the perspective of Game A, and vice versa.

If you're still not clear on what Game C is about, then that's good, because neither am I. That's definitely what Game C is about. Since we're clear on it not being clear, I've drawn this simple Venn diagram to show my understanding of how Games A, B, C, and the Jungle interact and overlap with each other:

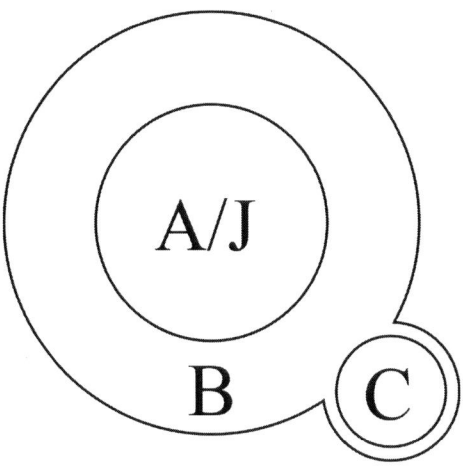

So many games. So little time. Maybe Game A yesterday, Game B today, Game C tomorrow, and before we know it, Game Over.

… Wanna play again?

Conclusion

Before I learned the art, a punch was just a punch, and a kick, just a kick. After I learned the art, a punch was no longer a punch, a kick, no longer a kick. Now that I understand the art, a punch is just a punch and a kick is just a kick.

— Bruce Lee

If I believed in agency, I'd congratulate you now on the accomplishment of making it this far. That back half is a real head scratcher. For anyone still scratching their heads and thinking "what do I do with this information?", I'd start by saying "there's that habit again…" and then I'd say "whatever you're going to end up doing." There's nothing to do… unless there is (and that takes care of itself too). Remember that I'm not talking about a change in the way things are. I'm talking about a perspective shift on what's already happening. You might as well surrender, because you already have.

I'm not saying that Game B is where it's at or that Game A is a problem that needs to be solved. If I could ensure one thing you took away from this book, it would be the following: There are other games. Try them and see what happens. Or don't. That's okay too. I'm in no way preaching or trying to convert you. I don't think it would be beneficial for society if everyone started viewing everything from a Game B perspective all the time. I'm almost certain it would be a disaster. Let's not do that. Unless we do. That's okay too.

I look around now, and things seem kind of disastrous when people become 100% steeped in Game A. Can we maybe take that down to around 95%? The deep version of this is that even this 100% disaster is 100% okay from a Game B perspective... But so is my desire to give the world a 5% break. It's *all* okay. I can't help my desire to share these insights, or my feeling that it would be beneficial for society if some of us could sometimes see some things from a Game B perspective. Being able to see both sides has been especially beneficial for me. Insert some woo woo nonsense here: Everything is okay... especially when it isn't. Trust the universe... especially when you don't.

The great irony I see is that someone trying their hardest not to go with the flow is still 100% going with the flow of not going with the flow. What a wonderful dance that is. Alan Watts says that when it comes to music, "one doesn't make the end of the composition the point of the composition. If that were so, the best conductors would be those who played fastest." If you were actually serious about winning at Game A, you'd play Game B, since it actually gets you to the desired destination. The moment I accepted that I was obviously already the best version of myself and couldn't possibly improve if I tried, my life began to improve in exactly the way I wanted it to before.

Christopher Robin: You don't need a balloon.

Winnie-the-Pooh: Well, I know I don't need one... but I would like one very, very much.

Christopher Robin (2018)

I feel compelled to address the apparent impracticality of This as a worldview when your life is staked on doing your way out of This. Who says Game A is so practical? It may sound terribly impractical to believe that neither "action," "agency," nor "doing" exist in the way that we think they do, and yet things appear to get done just fine from both perspectives. It would be easy to argue that much more gets done from a Game B perspective. One of the most discernible differences between the two games is that one of them assumes that the player is never good enough. Is this a practical advantage?

> All your crying don't do no good
> Come on up to the house
> Come down off the cross, we can use the wood
> You gotta come on up to the house

"Come On Up To The House" (Tom Waits)

In the excellent "Scientists Discussion #2" on the J. Krishnamurti - Official Channel on YouTube (I highly recommend watching all four parts if you have the time and interest), Krishnamurti suggests that one is only "stuck in a rut" if they identify themselves as such. He argues that our habit of identifying with images about ourselves is the root of our psychological disorders, asking "why do I want to identify myself?" One scientist counters that this process of identification is "a biological fact" and "not merely an illusion," noting how birds identify with their flocks and bees identify with their hives. Krishnamurti replies: "But bees don't kill themselves."

That scientist happened to be Rupert Sheldrake, who went on to author *The Science Delusion* (2012) thirty years later, in which he is critical of science as a belief system or a worldview. Boy, does that ever sound like a familiar game... Sheldrake advocates for science as an open-minded method of inquiry, or as Krishnamurti would urge us: "Let's investigate. Dig!" I've been criticized by intellectuals for pushing "pseudoscience" and "pseudophilosophy." Maybe this goofy woo woo stuff is more scientific and philosophical than it appears. Maybe not. Will you investigate for yourself?

I wouldn't claim to know which game is the most practical. Game B is not some source of divine capital T "Truth." It's simply a model of the world. But so is every other worldview. Even science (the source of some of our best models) is ultimately an attempt to describe and predict This, and not the other way around. C.S. Lewis said "to say that a stone falls to Earth because it is obeying a law makes it a man and even a citizen." In this case, the "law of gravity" is an attempt to describe the already happening behavior of a dropped stone. To me, "gravity" sounds more like a description of the painting of nature than like a law that nature obeys. I suppose the "description of gravity" doesn't quite sound as catchy.

When I was falling down this Game B rabbit hole in 2019, I'd often think about Tiger Woods, and the gravity that surrounded him while he dominated the sport of golf. When I talk about that fleeting zone of just doing vs trying, I always think of him. Master Yoda would be proud. It's hard to think of a better Game A slogan than Nike's "just do it," yet that's exactly what he did. He consistently made shots that made no sense. I remember commentators saying that he would "will the ball into the hole." Then he lost it, and spent more than a decade trying to be Tiger Woods again. But trying to be Tiger Woods isn't how he got the magic in the first place. It doesn't surprise me that his historic 2019 Masters win came when he finally gave up that game and embraced who he was in the moment.

I hope this book has primed you for some of your own magic moments and Game B insights. If I was successful in making a small crack, then you may have some pretty earth-shattering experiences in your future.

Maybe not. If you're ever wondering whether or not you see it, then you probably don't see it. It's uhhhhh not subtle. You'll know.

I've tried to avoid giving advice in this book. That said, if you do happen to start seeing it, and start riding some magical 10/10 experiences of your own, then I'd like to echo the advice my brother gave to me when he noticed that I was starting to see it:

> Like Tiger Woods, you will also "lose it" at some point. It might be tomorrow. It might be years from now. When you do, don't try to get it back. You don't need to get it back. There's nothing to get back. Losing it *is it*. It's some yin yang stuff, but basically the connectedness (the really deep one, that you may have felt by now) comes and goes like the weather. It has to. Because if you're always in the water, then you no longer feel wet. It will feel like you have really lost it. But once it comes back, you will realize that it being gone was just it in another form (quite a beautiful form at that). So when it happens, don't despair. Enjoy the new face of connectedness. And when it comes back, it will be that much more beautiful.

If you've gotten this far, and still feel like these ideas aren't useful to you, then I'd ask the obvious question: How is your current approach working out for you? If it's working out phenomenally, then that's phenomenal. Keep it up. I'll gladly shut up and smile as you toss this book in the fire.

Presumably you picked this book up looking for something, and you made it all the way to the end. Are you satisfied? If you simply wanted to listen to my ramblings as they washed over you like waves, then my guess is you're very satisfied. If you had a 10/10 experience or some mind blowing moments while reading it, then my guess is you're very satisfied (and I'll probably see you in the Jungle shortly). If you feel like what you were looking for isn't in here, then I 100% agree with you, and suspect it's not in any other book either. Need I remind you of the first line of the introduction?

Those who aren't satisfied will likely keep seeking the answer in other books, rereading this one, or urging me to write more. If so, then that would 0% be a problem from where I'm sitting. I wouldn't see them as wrong, nor as wasting their time. I'd actually find it hilarious, and see it as an incredible piece of performance art. For those of you keen on consuming extracurricular content, I've listed some songs and movies in the Media section that I feel have strong Game B themes and messages. The answer isn't in them either, but I'd rather you do just about anything other than reread this book for better comprehension. That said, it would be totally fine if you did, and I bone believe that. After all, it would be the Thing.

I'm beating a dead horse at this point, but I don't know how else to defend against you confusing my finger for the Moon. This collection of words is only a signpost, but it's pointing in a very intentional direction. I'm holding nothing back. When I say "I have nothing to teach you," I'm not being mystical or hiding something in an effort to get you to figure it out for yourself. I am not some conjurer of cheap tricks. And don't you dare think I'm trying to teach you that I have nothing to teach you. I'm not. TAKE. ME. AT. FACE. VALUE. I'm describing exactly what I mean. I can't be any more clear when I say:

Glossary

Game A: A progress-driven worldview so pervasive that its players see it as the only game in town.

Game B: The game we play before we learn Game A, and what presents itself as an alternative when we drop Game A.

Game C: Any game not easily recognizable as being motivated by typical Game A or Game B pursuits.

Fake Game B: The playing of Game B for Game A reasons (Game A by another name).

The Jungle: A common spiritual, existential, or philosophical crisis that occurs when we don't want to play Game A anymore, but we don't know how to stop.

The way out: The means of escaping the trap of the Jungle.

The Thing: A simplified twist on the ancient concept of the Tao meant to be more accessible for modern western culture.

The habit: Cycling on a perpetual belief that "I can do things" and that everything is a call to action.

10/10: A mystical or peak experience, often accompanied with a rush of endorphins and a sense of a natural high.

Sauce: A particularly wordy collection of concepts.

Ringwraith: Someone so lost in concepts that they can no longer engage with the phenomenon those concepts refer to.

Boxing: A mental process of constantly packaging, labeling, and filing sensory experiences away into their designated and delineated conceptual categories.

Wobble: A specific type of cognitive dissonance that occurs when the beliefs that someone built their understanding of the world on suddenly don't feel so solid.

Parachute: A thing that will save someone.

Hang Glider: A thing that will save someone once the parachute fails.

Flashlight Cranking: Manufacturing a fleeting sense of enlightenment in someone else by winding them up with wisdom.

Full expression: A state of absolute perfection.

Bone Belief: Any belief held so deeply that you 0% question it. It's not even on the table. It's 100% self-evident.

Cosmic want: The idea that you're always getting exactly what you want… You just have no idea what you want. This type of desire runs much deeper than conscious or surface-level desire.

God's problems: The kinds of problems you'd run into if you were an all-knowing, immortal, or unlimited being.

Media

Game B songs:

Colors Of The Wind
    (Judy Kuhn)
Jack's Lament
    (Danny Elfman)
Bold As Love
    (Jimi Hendrix)
Both Sides Now
    (Joni Mitchell)
Poor Man's Gold
    (Jamestown Revival)
Vienna
    (Billy Joel)
Nowhere To Be
    (The Bills)
Father And Son
    (Cat Stevens)
End Of The Line
    (The Traveling Wilburys)
Tan Te
    (Gong Linna)
Birds With Broken Wings
    (Ben Caplan)
Tell Me
    (Tom Waits)
I Don't Wanna Grow Up
    (Tom Waits)
The Southern Sea
    (Garth Stevenson)
Julep
    (Punch Brothers)
The River
    (Cat Clyde)
Hymn #35
    (Joe Pug)

Game B movies:

The Dark Knight (2008)
Lost in Translation (2003)
The Matrix (1999)
At Eternity's Gate (2018)
Collateral (2004)
My Octopus Teacher (2020)
Kung Fu Panda (2008)
The Nightmare Before Christmas (1993)

Special thanks to you.

You're the best version of yourself in my book.

Made in United States
North Haven, CT
19 July 2023

39278268R00098